Soldiers and Citizens
A Hundred Years of Armed Forces in Italy

BY:
Anna Maria Isastia

EDITORIAL DIRECTOR
Giovanna Naldi

ICONOGRAPHY DIRECTOR
Emanuela Sesti

ICONOGRAPHY RESEARCH
Gioconda Bartolotta
Daniela Cammilli

ART DIRECTOR AND DESIGN
Nina Peci - Media Studio, Florence

TRANSLATION
Erika Pauli - Studio Comunicare

PRINTING
Lito Terrazzi - Cascine del Riccio, Florence

© copyright 2000 by Fratelli Alinari
Largo Alinari, 15 Firenze
http://www.alinari.com
e-mail: info-more@alinari.it

ISBN 88-7292-330-1

THANKS TO
The Presidency of the Italian Republic
The Cabinet of the Italian Ministry of Defense
The Italian Defense General Staff
The Italian Army General Staff,
The Italian Navy General Staff,
The Italian Air Force General Staff,
The General Headquarters of the Italian
Carabinieri Corps
The A.N.R.P. (National Association of Veterans
from Imprisonment, Internment and the War
of Liberation) Center for Study, Documentation
and Research

Index

PRESENTATION FROM THE DEFENSE MINISTER OF THE ITALIAN REPUBLIC
Honorable Sergio Mattarella

A hundred years of history separate us from 1900 and if we look back on the past century, so dense with events that were often tragic and distressing, the close symbiosis between the story of the nation and the life of the Armed Forces, called upon to perform their role in the most delicate moments, comes to the fore.

A "brief century", the one that has just come to a close and in which the first fifteen years – up to World War I – are indissolubly tied to the way of life and thought of the preceding century and in which the last eleven years – from the fall of Berlin to the present – are part of the new epoch of globalization.

This book, which goes through 100 years of the military history of Italy, gives us rare and precious images of the Italian Armed Forces beginning with the early 1900s: young men wearing uniforms which look strange to modern eyes, the glorious protagonists of an epoch in which the young Kingdom of Italy – emerging from the Risorgimento – was affirming itself in all the world events. The Army, in many ways, personified the peasant and illiterate Italy of that time, newly unified, with all its social stratifications and regional differences, more decided and much graver than today, but determined to set out on the road to social and industrial transformation.

After the venture in Libya, which profoundly divided Italy, Europe moved on towards that unprecedented conflict of the "Great War". The deeds and enormous sacrifices of our soldiers and sailors, the exploits of the first aviators, have left an indelible mark on the collective memory: the Piave, the Grappa, Luigi Rizzo and his MAS, Francesco Baracca's fragile biplane have been the object of memorable pages of literature dear to the hearts of all Italians. The photographs presented here recall the heroic deeds of entire generations overwhelmed by the war.

Italy, which came victorious from that terrible trial of World War I, was never to be the same. A new solidarity between citizens of different extraction and provenience had matured in the trenches, a feeling of "homeland", in the sense of a collective value, had grown and taken root. In the post-war period the exaggerated exaltation of national values and revolutionary radicalism animated a difficult season of upheavals in which Bolshevism and the Fascist movements met with success. In the uneasy Europe of the 1920s and 30s, the Armed Forces appeared, as never before, as instruments of power and Fascist Italy was no exception, with its ventures in Spain, Ethiopia, Albania. Those were the years in which the Air Force, which had already come into the limelight in World War I, came into its own; these were the years in which flight progressed by leaps and bounds and was marked by great achievements for Italy such as the trans-Atlantic flight of a squadron of the young Air Force.

The Fascist dictatorial regime, after the alliance with Hitler's Germany, precipitated Italy into World War II. The Army, Navy and Air Force in those three hard years of war were sorely tried in the many operative stages and left inestimable evidence of their courage in Africa, Russia, the Balkans, the Mediterranean and even in the Atlantic as far as our submarines are concerned. In those dramatic events, however, a technological level and an operative vision not up to par with the epoch weighed heavily on Italy. The Armistice of September 8th dramatically marked the end of the war fought together with Germany, leaving the Armed Forces however without precise orders. The Resistance began, and starting with Porta San Paolo in Rome on September 10, 1943, soldiers and common citizens launched into the fight for national redemption and for liberty. A long series of combatants and martyrs marked its course which led, after twenty months of fighting, to the definitive defeat of Nazi-Fascism. These events also led to the rebirth of the Italian Armed Forces which, only three months after the Armistice, were crowned with success at Montelungo with the "Primo Reggimento Motorizzato" (First Motorized Regiment), a success which bore witness to the convinced participation of Italy in the Allied cause.

The second half of the century that has just come to an end belongs to the Republic. The democratic Constitution stresses the fact that defence of the Homeland is the sacred duty of the citizens, and affirms that Italy repudiates war as an instrument of offence to the liberty of other peoples and as a means of resolution of international controversies. The constitutional function of the Armed Forces, whose regulations must adapt themselves to the democratic spirit of the Republic, is recognized. In the long decades of the "cold war" in Italy and abroad, they participated in the defence of freedom and democracy. They gave their immediate and generous contribution in relief operations when natural calamities devastated the country, in the wake of a noble tradition of solidarity which as early as 1908, in the earthquake of Messina, had seen our military in the "front lines" in defence of the populations and in support of the subsequent reconstruction.

A new phase for the Italian Armed Forces began in the 1980s, above all after the fall of the Berlin wall, when they were called, ever more frequently, to participate in missions of peace beyond the national borders, instrument of an Italian foreign policy bound to the action of the international organizations, in support of legality. Lebanon, the Sinai, the Gulf and Kurdistan, Somalia, Mozambique, Bosnia, Albania, Kosovo and the entire Balkan theater, East Timor: they are all stages – by now known to the general public and well illustrated in this book – of an extraordinary commitment on the part of Italy, currently one of the leading contributing Countries, in terms of men, to the missions of peace.

The difference between the Armed Forces of 2000 and those of a century ago is immense, both in substance and in image, as this book so well demonstrates. The humble foot soldiers of 1900, sons of the poor Italy of the time and called up in the draft to serve the country often so far from home, have been replaced by the professional military of our days. A modern "battle dress" and an increasingly sophisticated individual and group armament have replaced the cartridge box, the mess-tin, the simple musket.

The Armed Forces of tomorrow, based on voluntary service, open to women, always faithful to the values of the constitution, are reflected in this new modern holography which, once and for all, replaces a vision tied to a "romantic" idea of the soldier and officer. At this stage of Italian and European history we have definitively left behind the "myths" of the demonstration of power which were such a large part of the dramatic century which has drawn to a close. Guarantees of efficiency, evidence of the motivations, and professional capacities now constitute the values which we wish to highlight in these years in which with courage, lucidity and determination, we place our military forces at the service of noble policies of stability, security and peace for a better future for all.

PREFACE FROM THE CHIEF OF STAFF FOR THE DEFENSE
General Mario Arpino

*O*ne must always reckon with one's own history. But reckoning with one's past is not simple when it is all recent history.

And perhaps it becomes even more difficult for a century like the twentieth, rent by epoch-making changes and in such contrast with the preceding century.

Such a clear-cut break in the analysis is, to say the least, subjective and a sign of wishful thinking but in history as in life, one needs points of reference in time which can simplify and help us better understand the course of events.

For the Italian Armed Forces these last hundred years – but also for all Italian citizens – have been anything but easy. We have had colonial wars, world wars and "hot and cold" ideological confrontations with the world split in two blocks. Other undeclared wars, in which our soldiers have however participated, shooting and being shot at, have euphemistically been called international police operations.

We have had diverse natural calamities such as, to cite only a few, the earthquakes in Messina and Umbria, Belice, Irpinia and the Friuli, floods in the Polesine and Florence, disasters such as the Vajont. Many remember the hard years of economical reconstruction, the difficult years of terrorism, which served as backdrop for the achievements of our soldiers.

Currently we have the humanitarian peace operations in Lebanon, Albania, Somalia, in the countries of the former Yugoslavia or in distant East Timor.

In these last hundred years, the Italian Armed Forces have always been present in the life of the nation. Often, but perhaps not always, we have covered ourselves with glory, perhaps we have not always been on the right side, but by the same token our country has not always made the best choices either. Even so the tribute we have paid in lives and sacrifices should underscore our many merits and outweigh our inevitable errors. On the other hand, who never makes a mistake? Indeed, speaking of history, of our history, already means we accept ourselves as we are and as we were, serenely, for good and bad, so that we can improve, will not repeat the same errors.

It is moreover all to easy to pass judgment a posteriori, with different knowledge and awareness, and, as the saying goes, "hindsight is easier than foresight".

This century comes to end for the Italian armed Forces with a surge of the new, with new commitments, new missions, with a new relationship to society and a new relationship within our organization, thanks also to the entrance of women. It is surely chance, but an auspicious one, that the author of this work is a woman, Professor Anna Maria Isastia, whom I would like to thank for her meticulous condensation of the many events in our history. As a scholar she had already dedicated many articles to particularly important topics such as voluntary female military service in Italy and women in the Italian Armed Forces.

This book is a useful reflection and meditation on what has been, to give us a greater awareness of future challenges, a key to the interpretation of the past for a better understanding of the present. Years of hard work will be needed as we face the tasks in store for us and the changes under way. But I believe that the Armed Forces can look to the future with confidence. And I share this confidence, both as a citizen and, as a soldier who is alas no longer young.

Introduction

*I*n the old films, the leading man all the girls fell in love with was often wearing an elegant Army or Navy officer's uniform. Or if he was in the Air Force, he was probably wearing a pilot's outfit with goggles, jumping on board his fighter or biplane. He might be seen in the parlors ready to leave on some mission, but rarely did he appear in war. When women went to the movies they wanted to fall in love with a handsome soldier who looked like Roberto Villa or even Fosco Giachetti, but they had no desire to see tragedy or blood. The simple soldier was not nearly as romantic and was rarely a hero. His role was generally limited to caricature, with knickerbockers and a forage cap. The girls snubbed him, unless it was Nino Manfredi in 'L'avventura di un soldato' where the adventure took place silently and swiftly as the train passed through a tunnel. In Italy war films were never a genre, as in the United States, and their purpose was on the whole, as in Rosi's 'Uomini contro', and even Monicelli's 'La grande guerra', to denounce the futility, stupidity and cruelty of conflicts. Men in uniform have never been as popular in Italy as they are now, committed, thank heaven, not to war but to missions of peace. One reason is also that television, in keeping with its job, in reporting their magnificent work in Bosnia or in Kurdistan, in Somalia and in Kosovo, does not tell quite all the truth so as not to alarm the soldier's relatives, so as not to leave too grim a picture with the audience. Television always shows the soldier in a perfect uniform, young and handsome wearing a beret or helmet, and coming to the aid of civilians, above all smiling children or weeping old ladies, helping to rebuild, distributing provisions, receiving flowers from pretty girls. Television is not always that careful about keeping us safe from the horrors, as in the case of the two Israeli soldiers who were linched. But luckily when dealing with our peacekeeping boys in the most hopeless sites in the world, they give us an Italian story of youth and devotion, of sacrifice and heroism. Up to a few years ago this story seemed to be only male, allowed only men to wear the uniform, perhaps to protect the women, perhaps because women were thought to be more fragile, unsuitable. While however women were the tragic and defenceless victims, they then showed their true side as unarmed heroines defending their homes, children, villages, from destruction and massacres. It is said that women do not want war, they want only peace, and therefore why should they wear a uniform. But beginning with spring of the year 2000, it is for peace, that the Italian women are admitted to the Naval, Air Force and Military academies.

Natalia Aspesi

The Armed Forces in the Giolitti Period

The Armed Forces are the fruit of the society of which they are the expression and mirror the values and behavior of that society. Instrument of decisions regarding peace and war, they are particularly sensitive to the political conditions in which their action takes shape.

In the early twentieth century Italy was still a young nation, barely forty years old. The military traditions of the old pre-unification States still lingered on in the Armed Forces and the regional differences were still strongly felt. Officers were well thought of socially and were honored drawing room guests. Special treatment was reserved for them with discounts for the theater and with attendant orderlies. For the landed middle classes the military career was a way of rising up in society.

A junior officer could not marry unless his wife had a military dowry, that is unless she had property which allowed her not to be a burden economically on her husband. The natural consequences were of course a plethora of marriages celebrated only in the church, with all the ensuing problems.

Non-commissioned officers were draftees or voluntary enlistees who signed up for at least five years and were not highly thought of.

Beginning in 1861, one of the results of conscription, after the unification of Italy, was an overwhelming failure to report for military service, above all in the southern regions where there was no cultural preparation at all in this regards. In a peasant society the long term of service was highly detrimental to the family economy for it took needed manpower from the land. To avoid conscription, some purposely mutilated themselves, many deserted, and suicides were not unusual.

On the other hand being rejected by the Armed Forces as unfit for military service soon came to be considered a dishonor, a sign of scarce virility. A sort of conscription ritual was thus created, celebrated in the country as a passage from adolescence to adulthood.

To lighten the burden of military service, the Italian middle classes frequently took advantage of an option offered by General Cesare Ricotti's reform of the army and which stayed on the books until 1920. One could volunteer for a year, paying two thousand lire, a way of ensuring the lower echelons without costs on the German model. It was actually none other than a privilege that permitted less taxing military obligations to be fulfilled close to home.

In the meanwhile the development of industry in the north led to an increase in the number of southerners who enlisted, as was the case in the civil services. Agrarian income was dropping, there were few jobs available and the young men of the south ended up by embracing the military career.

In 1910 the term of service was reduced to two years for the entire contingent of 120,000 men, part of whom in times of peace were involved in maintaining the public order.

The interventions of the Italian Armed Forces when natural calamities such as fire, earthquakes or floods struck were countless. Massive aid was provided by the Armed Forces to the Calabrian and Sicilian populations who were awakened in the early hours of December 28, 1908 by a violent earthquake which destroyed the city of Messina and seriously damaged Reggio Calabria. Tens of thousands died, many more were wounded. Italian, Russian and English war units navigating in the Mediterranean immediately headed for Messina and all the Services and specialized troops of the Army took part in the rescue activities. About 20,000 soldiers were deployed on the territory in the most difficult moments: from the Alpine troops to the Carabinieri, the Engineers

MESSINA EARTHQUAKE, 1908. PHOTO LUCA COMERIO. Italian Army personnel digging among the rubble *(Fratelli Alinari Museum of the History of Photography, Florence)*

Corps to the infantry to the Excise and Revenue police (Guardia di Finanza). The Navy made its entire fleet available for the transportation of troops, food and aid of all kinds, hospital units, equipment for the military engineers, as well as transferring the wounded and refugees to hospitals and assembly centers elsewhere. It was not until the summer of 1909 that the Armed Forces were replaced by the civilian organs of reconstruction.

FROM ADWA TO TRIPOLI

After the painful rout of 1896 at Adwa in the Horn of African, Crispi handed in his resignation as prime minister and the Italian colonial program was abandoned.

In 1900 however Italy was present in China with a contingent of infantrymen, one of Bersaglieri (a corps of sharpshooters) and mixed personnel for a total of 83 officers, 1822 troops and 178 quadrupeds joined by the sailors of the units stationed in the area. The Tientsin concession was obtained thanks to the Italian intervention. It was an international expedition to free the Europeans, besieged in their legation quarters in Peking by the Boxers who were revolting against the presence of Westerners.

The Italian political scene in the first fifteen years of the century was dominated by Giolitti, a discerning statesman, adaptable and strong but whose pragmatic vision, far from utopias and extremism, was challenged by large sectors of the country. "We are in a period of formation, we have great problems to solve which directly concern the economic, social and political life of the Country" Giolitti affirmed to the House "we must provide for the rehabilitation of the South, we must improve working class conditions, for not all in Italy have achieved that level of well-being which it is our duty to procure for them. We must also see to public education, it is our duty to promote a fiscal reform and this is all attainable only if we pursue a policy of peace".

The international situation was however increasingly strained and Germany and Austria-Hungary, Italy's allies, did not look with a favorable eye on the renewed relationships with France and England. The new Austrian chief of staff, General Conrad von Hoetzendorf, was openly hostile to Italy and this made it imperative to fortify the northeastern frontiers in addition to strengthening defences against France.

Giolitti was forced to increase military spending, so that the War Ministry and the Chief of Staff could reorganize the army and the navy. Pay, meals, barracks lodgings were improved. The infantry and cavalry divisions adopted machine guns. Motorization of the army was begun.

In 1910 the first flight training school was founded and the first allocation of funds for the building of airplanes was approved. There were so many requests from the military that neither the governmental nor the private industries were able to meet them all.

The African defeats were forgotten and Enrico Corradini's theory on the division between "plutocratic nations" and "proletarian nations", those which had more inhabitants than economical resources, became popular.

At the end of 1910 the Nationalist movement was set up as an association and began an incessant campaign in favor of the conquest of Libya, which was part of the Ottoman empire, in full agreement with the moderate Catholic groups linked to Vatican finances and the Banco di Roma, already involved in the economic penetration of Libya.

While the press praised the vaunted fertility of the African country to the skies, a country which could become the new homeland for many Italians no longer forced to emigrate, the Moroccan crisis of summer 1911 counseled the Italian government to substantiate the agreements which recognized Italian interests in Libya. When the war broke out on September 29th, the Navy and the landing infantry were forced to weigh anchor without the expedition corps which did not join them until October 11th under the command of Caneva. The constitution of a fleet of airplanes was ordered on September 28th. They were used for reconnaissance missions, bombing and cooperation from the air, the first time ever that planes were employed in a war.

Tripoli, Tobruk, Derna, Benghazi, Homs were occupied immediately but, after the revolt of Tripoli, the Italians found themselves fighting a hostile population. On November 5th Giolitti proclaimed the annexation of Libya, but Arab guerrilla warfare, fostered by the Turks, continued. In the early months of 1912 the forces were increased to about a hundred thousand, all machine gun divisions were sent to Africa, new divisions were set up, warehouses and depots were emptied. Thaon de Revel had the forts and the port of Beirut bombed. Millo tried to force the Dardanelle Strait with torpedo boats.

In October 1912 the peace treaty with Turkey was signed, but when World War I broke out there were still 50,000 soldiers in Libya. The war had cost Italy 1,430 dead on the field, 4,250 wounded and 1,948 victims of mortal diseases. Rome now had a great colony in northern Africa: an immense "box of sand". Italy's position in the Mediterranean had also been strengthened by the conquest of Rhodes and the Dodecanese Islands by the Navy.

ITALY ON THE EVE OF THE GREAT WAR

The war in Libya radicalized the political contrasts while social tensions were embittered by the economic slump. The first elections with universal male suffrage of November 1913 brought the Nationalists to the Chamber for the first time, the Socialists increased their seats, but above

MESSINA EARTHQUAKE, 1908. Bersaglieri troops of the Royal Army lending aid on the site of the disaster. *(Fratelli Alinari Museum of the History of Photography, Florence)*

***ITALO-TURKISH WAR,
TRIPOLI. FEBRUARY 1912.***
210 A trench mortar.
*(Historical Bureau
of the Army General
Staff, Rome)*

all the Catholic component, which up to then had been purposely absent, became significant. The majority was still in the hands of Liberals of various degrees, but a left wing in which the revolutionary currents had taken the lead over the reform currents was in clear opposition to the conservative right wing, reinforced by the Nationalists and the moderate clerical party.

In May of 1914 Giolitti resigned and Antonio Salandra, a right-wing liberal, formed a conservative government.

A month later, a demonstration in Ancona ended with the death of three anti-militant demonstrators. Republicans and Socialists responded with a wave of strikes and riots, some even of an insurrectional nature. The one called the "red week" had just been put down when the war broke out.

While the war in Libya had attracted many Italians to the Armed Forces and new sectors of the population had discovered patriotism, it had damaged and thrown the rearmament program out of kilter. Financially the cost was enormous: 1,300 million lire.

General Pollio, chief of staff, did all he could to reassure the Allies, confirming the intentions of Italy to transport an army to the Rhine in case of a Franco-German conflict. On December 5, 1912, the Triple Alliance was renewed, joining Italy with Germany and the Habsburg Empire, and a naval Convention was added in June 1913.

It was fate that General Pollio died on the eve of the outbreak of the war. He was replaced by General Luigi Cadorna.

ITALO-TURKISH WAR, 1911-12. Capt. Piazza's Blériot aircraft and, in the background, a 'Draken' observation balloon under preparation. The Blériot was the first aircraft in the world to undertake a war flight. *(Air Force General Staff – Audiovisual production center, Rome)*

***Italo-Turkish war,
1911-12.*** Dismasted
brig 'Caval Marino' used
for the transportation
of a 'Draken' captive
reconnaissance balloon.
The 'Draken' helped the
ships aim artillery fire
before a landing.
*(Air Force General Staff
– Audiovisual production
center, Rome)*

***Italo-Turkish war,
1911-12.*** Capt. Moizo's
Nieuport in Tripoli. This
plane, like the Blériot,
flew one of the first war
flights in the world.
*(Air Force General Staff
– Audiovisual production
center, Rome)*

ITALO-TURKISH WAR,
1911-12. PHOTO BRUNO
MINIATI. Military
photographic sector at
work. *(Fratelli Alinari*
Museum of the History
of Photography – Miniati
archive, Florence)

***ITALO-TURKISH WAR,
1911-12.*** Men landing
pieces of artillery.
*(Air Force General Staff
– Audiovisual production
center, Rome)*

ITALO-TURKISH WAR,
1911-12. Men landing
pieces of artillery.
*(Air Force General Staff
– Audiovisual production
center, Rome)*

Italo-Turkish war, 1911-12. Photo Luca Comerio. Line-up of Army trucks. The first logistic and tactical mass use of transportation vehicles in war operations was in the Libyan war. The experience of the Italo-Turkish conflict turned out to be very useful in the logistic field in the course of World War I. *(Historical Bureau of the Navy, Rome)*

ITALO-TURKISH WAR, 1911-12. PHOTO LUCA COMERIO. Airships in the hangars. Used for the first time in the Italo-Turkish war, the airships with which both the army and the navy were equipped, were used for aerial reconnaissance, photographic spotting and bombing. They became obsolete after World War I.
(Historical Bureau of the Navy, Rome)

LIBYA, APRIL 1913.
Italian troops
disembarking at
Tolmetta during the
Italian occupation of
Libya. *(Fratelli Alinari
Museum of the History
of Photography,
Florence)*

World War I

On June 28, 1914 Francis Ferdinand, Archduke of Austria, was assassinated at Sarajevo and on July 28th, with the full support of Germany, but without consulting Italy, Austria declared war on Serbia. In a few days all the great powers were at war.

Italy however declared its neutrality. Not only was the thirty-year alliance stipulated with Austria solely defensive, but it also contrasted with governmental policy. In the months to follow the government was under the illusion it could entrust the Armed Forces with the role of simply supporting political and diplomatic initiatives. A deep-rooted anti-Austrian tendency prevailed in the upper echelons of the army, while the Anglophile current was strong in the navy.

Hopes were for a war limited to the conquest of the irredentist territories, brief and limited in costs. The only one convinced of the need for total mobilization, in open contrast with the politicians, was Cadorna.

On April 26, 1915, after months of secret negotiations, Italy signed the London treaty joining her to France and Russia along with England. On May 4th Italy denounced the Triple Alliance, and on May 24th went to war against Austria. Rome asked for the Trentino and the Tyrol up to Brenner, Istria and the Dalmatian coast.

The majority of the nation was neutralist, but the interventionist minority including intellectuals such as the futurist Marinetti, poets such as D'Annunzio, politicians such as Mussolini made itself heard.

The government and King Victor Emmanuel III wanted a war that would complete the campaigns of the Risorgimento, and the attainment of the natural confines with a rapid conflict. This was the great illusion of those years, shared by all the armies and which failed everywhere. The small war was to become the Great War.

The mobilized army could count on 31,000 officers, 1,058,000 troops, 216,000 quadrupeds. The Air Force consisted of fifteen squadrons of planes.

Most of the 600 kilometers of frontier between Italy and Austria ran along the hills and mountains of which the Austrians controlled the ridges and peaks. The Italian offensive was centered on the Isonzo River front which permitted both defence and offense.

A convinced theoretician of frontal attack, in three years Cadorna launched a long series of exhausting offensives along the Isonzo River which cost hundreds of thousands of lives.

The Austrians answered in May of 1916 with the *Strafexpedition*, a large offensive which, after an initial overwhelming success, failed due to the persistent resistance of the Italian army. The Italian troops reached Gorizia on August 9, 1916, the first real success of the war.

Meanwhile, in June 1916 the Salandra government fell and with the constitution of the government of national unity, presided over by Boselli, the second phase of the conflict began. Italy declared war on Germany as well and admitted that it was now participating in a total war. Endeavors were made to involve the nation in what by then was obviously a "great war", and there were attempts at creating links between the soldiers in the trenches and the home front.

In the collective memory World War I is represented by the trenches and tunnels, dug in the mud or rock, in the worst imaginable sanitary conditions. The trench was a place to wait and hold out in a nerve-racking war of position for soldiers on all fronts. A strip of no man's land marked by barbed wire fences lay between opposing trenches. Veterans tell of the anguish of a life where

ROME, NOVEMBER 4, 1921. FOTO. D. ANDERSON, Arrival of the body of the unknown soldier in Rome. The procession moves along Via Nazionale on its way to the Altar of the Homeland in Piazza Venezia.
(Alinari Archives – Anderson archive, Florence)

tedium alternated with deadly assaults, describing the terrible resignation and passivity of the many soldiers who went out against the machine guns, obeying commands they could not understand. The situation in the trenches improved with time, but rotations were still a problem.

This new type of war obviously led to the modernization and development of the industries. Profits escalated from 6.3% to 16.5% for the iron and steel industry and from 8% to 30% for the automobile sector.

This impetuous development was accompanied by an increase in government intervention in all sectors of civilian life. New tasks and roles entrusted to a rapidly growing bureaucracy ensued. The relationship between public and private changed and those between politics and the economy were modified.

For the first time in Italy the economic world and the military power met.

The need to coordinate the requests of the military ministries and to program industrial efforts, ensuring raw materials and manpower, led to a series of measures which went by the name of "industrial mobilization".

The Italian army, with an offensive war on its mind, was unprepared for a new tykpe of offensive. It unexpectedly collapsed on October 24, 1917 when the Austrians, reinforced by seven German divisions, attacked the Italian lines on the Isonzo River and broke through near Caporetto, rapidly advancing into Friuli.

In the course of the war the Germans replaced a rigid with an elastic defence and perfected a new plan of offensive battle which was successful above all expectations. While the enemy advance was brought to a halt, at extremely high cost, on the Piave River and on Monte Grappa, a new Government of National Unity was being formed. It was presided over by Vittorio Emanuele Orlando and the watchword was that the native land was in danger. Cadorna, who was Piedmontese, was replaced by the Neapolitan Armando Diaz, less inclined to indiscriminate repression and more aware of what the soldiers needed.

The soldiers rallied and succeeded in resisting on the line of the Piave and the Grappa. The importance of financing a real propaganda structure to explain the reasons for the war to the soldiers at the front and to the Italians, finally hit home. Supreme Headquarters sent hundreds of photographers to capture every phase of the war on film.

A massive campaign of persuasion was directed at the troops, all the more effective because the war had become defensive. Appeals to patriotism and the duty to resist made inroads. The new Commander in Chief Diaz also realized that the well-being of the troops was of fundamental importance for the morale of the Armed Forces. A government policy of assistance to the families of the soldiers was begun and servicemen were granted an insurance policy.

In the long years of the war, the Navy did its utmost to obtain military and political control in the Adriatic, coordinating the activities of the French and English units involved in the operations.

Even though there were no real naval battles between the Italians and Austrians, their efforts extended to the western Mediterranean and their activities included escorting convoys bringing in supplies. It was also thanks to the Navy that the Serbian army was rescued, and the retreating troops were transported from the eastern coast to the coast of Puglia. The lighter units, submarines, MAS and torpedo boats, were particularly active and included operations which employed completely new types of naval crafts. Outstanding were the actions of Rizzo with the MAS (motorboats anti-submarine). In December 1917 he forced the port of Trieste, torpedoing

STABILIMENTO ANSALDO, CORNIGLIANO, 1918.
Production of a 381/40 cannon
(*Fratelli Alinari Museum of the History of Photography, Florence*)

the battleships *Wien* (which sank) and *Budapest*. In February 1918, with D'Annunzio aboard, Rizzo arrived in the harbor of Buccari and attacked a few ocean liners, to no avail. On June 10, 1918, near Premuda, he attacked the Austrian fleet as it was leaving Pola for an action in the southern Adriatic and succeeded in sinking the battleship *Santo Stefano*.

After a few actions against the port of Pola using special units to pass over the obstructions, the medical Captain Paolucci and the naval engineer Major Rossetti succeeded in penetrating the port of Pola with a special craft on the night of October 31st to November 1, 1918. They attacked and sank the battleship *Viribus Unitis*. This was the last act of the war in the Adriatic.

The activities of the aviation units began with photographic reconnaissance flights over the zone of Podgora. Monfalcone was bombed on May 25th. In April 1916, Major Francesco Baracca obtained the first Italian fighter plane victory downing an Austrian plane in the skies of Medeuzza. The operations of the aerial forces during the war developed in various ways. The pilots multiplied their reconnaissance and photographic flights. On February 19, 1918, they bombed and machine/gunned the railroad stations of Bolzano and Innsbruck. In the battle of the Piave of June 1918 the massive use of fighter planes and bombers played an important part in the enemy withdrawal. On August 9th , ten Italian planes flew over Vienna launching tricolor handbills. The idea was Gabriele D'Annunzio's. The Italian aviation actively participated in the battle of Vittorio Veneto.

In the war years an enormous industrial effort was made to bring men and means up to the new needs. When the armistice was signed, there were 1758 planes and 26 dirigibles in active service on the Italian, French and Greco-Albanian fronts.

left:
WORLD WAR I. CORPS OF VOLONTEERS.
Departure from Milan of the Btg Volontari Ciclisti Lombardi. *(Historical Bureau of the Army General Staff, Rome)*

WORLD WAR I. PHOTO BRUNO MINIATI. Italian army personnel in the trenches.
Note the metal nets as defense against the launching of hand grenades.
(Fratelli Alinari Museum of the History of Photography – Miniati archive, Florence)

World War I.
Farman type 1914
reconnaissance aircraft
in the air.
(*Air Force General Staff
– Audiovisual production
center, Rome*)

below:
World War I.
Francesco Baracca with
the SPAD VII aircraft
with which he won his
last victories
(*Air Force General Staff
– Audiovisual production
center, Rome*)

On October 24, 1918, Diaz launched an offensive on the front of the Piave and Grappa. Italy closed the war with the battle of Vittorio Veneto. On November 3rd, Udine, Trento and Trieste were occupied by the Italian troops while the armistice was being signed at Villa Giusti.

About half of the Italian males between 18 and 40 years of age contributed to the victory, for a total of 4,200,000 men at the front. There were 500,000 casualties; another 500,000 remained invalid; 600,000 fell prisoners and 100,000 never returned home.

The Armed Forces had shown they were solid and compact and could count on the obedience of the soldiers, although there were some, as happens in all armies, who protested and refused.

WORLD WAR I. Line-up
of Farman type 1914
reconnaissance aircraft
*(Air Force General Staff
– Audiovisual production
center, Rome)*

right:
WORLD WAR I. Front
line first aid station.
*(Historical Bureau
of the Army General
Staff, Rome)*

WORLD WAR I. Navy
infantry in the trenches
ready to attack.
*(Historical Bureau of the
Navy, Rome).*

WORLD WAR I.
Carabinieri equipped for mountain fighting.
(Historical Bureau of the General Headquarters of the Carabinieri Corps, Rome).

WORLD WAR I. Piece
of 65 mm mountain
artillery in emplacement
on the Alps.
The piece could be
taken apart for
packsaddle
transportation on mules.
(*Historical Bureau
of the Army General
Staff, Rome*)

WORLD WAR I, MAY 1916. Rescuing those wounded in the Strafexpedition. *(Archives of the Historical Bureau of the Army General Staff, Rome)*

***WORLD WAR I, AUGUST
9, 1916. PHOTO BRUNO
MINIATI.*** Entry of the
Italian troops in Gorizia,
after the victorious 6th
battle of the Isonzo.
*(Fratelli Alinari Museum
of the History of
Photography – Miniati
archive, Florence)*

World War I. Armed pontoon with two 190/45 naval cannons and service personnel at the guns. Used up to 1915, the armed pontoons were used particularly in the Venetian lagoon to defend Venice after the defeat of Caporetto. Large, medium or small caliber artillery was set up on the armed pontoon, depending on the number of pieces mounted. The pieces of artillery mounted on the pontoon were originally meant to be installed on board a Royal Navy unit. The armed pontoon was towed by a tug-boat to avoid the fire of the Austrian counterbattery. One of its tasks was that of coastal defense but priority use was for firing on land objectives. *(Historical Bureau of the Navy, Rome).*

S. E. Cadorna passa in rivista una compagnia del..... Reggimento fanteria.

above:
WORLD WAR I.
Picket presenting arms in honor of General Cadorna in the course of an inspection at the front. *(Fratelli Alinari Museum of the History of Photography, Florence)*

WORLD WAR I, PASUBIO, WINTER 1916-17.
Snow communication trench towards Palom (m. 2215). In the course of World War I the troops at the front had to face the rigors of the climate and the adversities of the mountain, fighting on unexplored mountain peaks. *(Historical Bureau of the Army General Staff, Rome)*

WORLD WAR I.
"Mass on the Pasubio.
snow altar." *(Historical
Bureau of the Army
General Staff, Rome)*

left:
WORLD WAR I. PHOTO BRUNO MINIATI. Piave.
Advance scout scanning
the enemy positions.
*(Fratelli Alinari Museum
of the History of
Photography – Miniati
archive, Florence)*

**WORLD WAR I. PHOTO
BRUNO MINIATI.** Hauling
of a 75 mm Mod. 906
campaign cannon.
*(Fratelli Alinari Museum
of the History of
Photography – Miniati
archive, Florence)*

Trieste, December 10, 1917. Gold medal being awarded to Commander Luigi Rizzo for sinking the Austrian battleship Wien. He will also be decorated with another gold medal the following year for sinking another enemy battleship, the *Santo Stefano*.
(Historical Bureau of the Navy, Rome)

***Italian ammunitions
factory, c. 1918.
Photo Giancarlo
dall'Armi.*** Casting
division. *(Fratelli Alinari
Museum of the History
of Photography –
Falzone collection,
Florence)*

WORLD WAR I, AUGUST 9, 1918. Line-up of SVA airacraft at the Aviation Field of S. Pelagio, Padua. *(Historical Bureau of the Army General Staff, Rome)*

WORLD WAR I.
Italian naval unit entering the harbor in Fiume welcomed by the jubilant crowd.
(Historical Bureau of the Navy, Rome)

Trento, November 3, 1918. The first R.R. Carabinieri arriving in the city.
(Historical Bureau of the General Headquarters of the Carabinieri Corps, Rome)

CEREMONY COMMEMORATING THE VICTORY OF WORLD WAR I.
(Fratelli Alinari Museum of the History of Photography, Florence)

The Difficult Postwar

On January 18, 1919, the peace conference opened in Versailles. The presence of America and the disappearance of the Austrian empire profoundly changed the situation which had led to the signing of the London Pact, to which the president of the council Orlando and the foreign minister Sonnino remained faithful, despite the opinion to the contrary of Bissolati.

Italy came out of the war stronger than before. She had the Trentino and Friuli and obtained her frontier at Brenner. It had however become difficult to ask for the territories promised in 1915 when no government could have foreseen the collapse of the Habsburg empire. The Italian government was committed to defending agreements superceded by the new state of affairs, and as a result public opinion in Italy was hostile to its former allies and the ruling class.

There was talk of a "mutilated victory".

On the other hand the principle of nationality, used by the Italians in asserting their rights to obtain Fiume, created real problems in Istria and Dalmatia where the Slavs were a majority, but which Italy claimed on the basis of the London Pact.

In September 1919 a few rebel military detachments, together with a group of volunteers, under the command of the poet Gabriele D'Annunzio, occupied the city of Fiume, inhabited by a majority of Italians but under international control after the dissolution of Austria-Hungary. The question of Fiume raised diplomatic, military and political problems and contributed to the fall of liberal Italy. The breakdown of discipline was serious; the fracture between a small group of young officials and the upper echelons was a matter of concern.

The occupation of Fiume by D'Annunzio's Legionaries was discussed with the Yugoslavian delegates. The Treaty of Rapallo established a special status for the city. To clear out Fiume, Giolitti mobilized the army and the navy and bombed the Government headquarters. There were also a few skirmishes on the land front. The city was annexed to Italy in 1924 with the Nettuno agreements.

Italy obtained various islands of the Quarnaro and its sovereignty over Zara was recognized.

Once the armistice was signed, demobilization began. The decision to discharge a million men in two months was not the best way of guaranteeing tranquility to the public at a time of strong social tensions which the arrival of so many veterans seeking work could only aggravate.

The half promises made to the soldiers of lands to be assigned to the peasants, were in the end limited to modest measures for the veterans. Too little for people who were coming back home without jobs. There was considerable unemployment among the officers too, which entailed a variety of political consequences.

By the autumn of 1920 the army had shrunk to 200,000 men (there were 3,760,000 when the war ended).

FIUME, DECEMBER 1918.
Inter-alliance police
*(Historical Bureau of the
General Headquarters of
the Carabinieri Corps,
Rome)*

preceding page,
above:
FLORENCE, 1920's.
Pignone workers
on strike.
(Alinari Archives - Villani
archive, Bologna)

FIUME, OCTOBER 1,
1919. Gabriele
d'Annunzio during the
venture of Fiume
(Fratelli Alinari Museum
of the History of
Photography, Florence)

MARCH ON ROME,
28 OCTOBER 1922.
The Quadrumvirate.
(Fratelli Alinari Museum
of the History of
Photography, Florence)

Armed Forces and Fascism

The post-war period was marked by polemics on the political evaluation and management of military operations. The extreme left was violently anti-military, international and anti-patriotic and those who had fought and suffered reacted negatively. It is not surprising that faced with increasing hostility to the military milieu, some of the officers sympathized with Fascism "interpreted by the military authorities as an ideal movement for restoring national power, making any excess appear lawful and amply justified by the purpose to which the action of these recent organizations is directed".

These were the words in a telegram sent by the ministry of the interior and made public by De Felice.

The General Staff was extremely energetic in blocking any pro-fascist stand and in fighting the spread of Fascist propaganda within the army and among the Carabinieri (particularly pre-occupying in the area of the Corps in Bari, Venezia Giulia, and above all Tuscany).

A reform of the Armed Forces inspired by the concept of an armed nation was proposed (short term of service in times of peace and mobilization of the entire populace in times of war). This was Giuseppe Garibaldi's democratic ideal. It was taken up by the *combattentisti*, the national political movement founded by ex-servicemen after World War I, by early Fascism in 1919, and by Catholics and Giolittiani, but it went no further.

According to Ceva, there was a rapid symbiosis between Fascism and the Armed Forces on a medium-low level, but when the Crown seemed to oppose Fascism, the army immediately followed suit. However when the King gave in, the alliance was immediately consolidated. The Blackshirts paraded in Rome at the end of 1922 before the King, Diaz and Thaon de Revel, who were immediately nominated ministers of War and of the Navy in the first Mussolini government.

Once in power, Mussolini attempted to make the army Fascist, but then he took great care to preserve its neutrality even against personalities such as Italo Balbo and Rodolfo Graziani.

In 1923 the Voluntary Militia for National Security (milizia volontaria per la sicurezza nazionale MVSN) was instituted, an autonomous armed force, upon which the military cast a diffident eye, to keep the *squadristi*, or members of the Fascist action squad, in line.

Mussolini was interested in keeping the army under control and seeing to it that military spending did not weigh too heavily on the budget. He obtained both of these aims by nominating Pietro Badoglio chief of staff.

Mussolini had a new system of regulations for the army drawn up in 1926. The size of the military apparatus and expenses were reduced in order to balance the budget. With this system of 1926 the army acquired a fixed staff. The Carabinieri continued to carry out their traditional tasks as military police for the Armed Forces, with the repression of common crime and maintenance of public order. They were employed particularly in the campaign against the Sicilian mafia, in the period of the prefect Mori, in the fight against Sardinian banditism in 1927-29 and in the intervention after the earthquake of Vulture in 1930.

STRATEGIES AND CONFLICTS IN MUSSOLINI'S POWER POLITICS

The Italy of the1920s did not have great ambitions. The kingdom of Yugoslavia, set up by French diplomacy in an anti-Italian function, was on the eastern border. The Italian operations

TRANS - ATLANTIC ROME - CHICAGO FLIGHT OF 1933. Formation flying over the city of Chicago and Lake Michigan of the S 55 X aircraft at the end of the transatlantic flight. The aircraft were distinguished by squadron with the national colors. Those of the Balbo squadron were black *(Air Force General Staff – Audiovisual production center, Rome)*

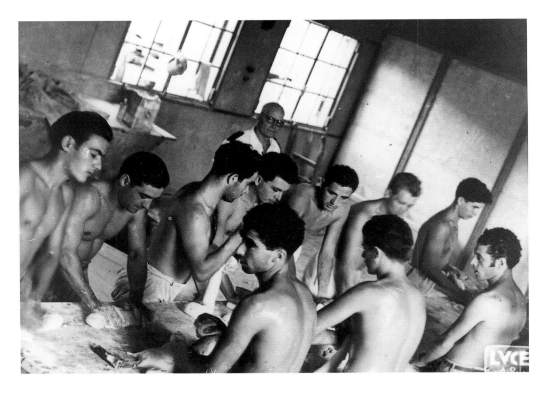

plan was oriented towards a war to be fought in the Alpine circle.

Italy had no intentions of antagonizing the English or French navies in the Mediterranean. In the early postwar period and up to World War II the Italian navy was interested primarily in defending the program of acquisitions of the Istrian and Dalmatian territories.

Up to the conquest of Ethiopia, Mussolini's involvement in military questions was limited, even if he held the military ministries from 1925 to 1929 and then again in 1933. He considered spending for the army unproductive, but wanted the military authorities to support his affirmations of efficiency.

Marshal Badoglio guaranteed control of the army to Mussolini and loyalty of the Armed Forces to the King. It was this role which permitted Badoglio to remain chief of staff for all of fifteen years (1925-1940).

After 1930, army expenses were further reduced by the economic crisis and the temporary improvement of relationships with France. Costs of the personnel were the highest, while those relative to the "equipment, means and preparations for war" were irrelevant. Things were different for the Navy and the Air Force.

The situation in the early postwar period led to the restructuring of the Navy apparatus. There were now five arsenals. La Spezia, Naples, Taranto, Venice and Pola. In 1925 a program for naval construction was begun (fast cruisers, destroyers, submarines) which amounted to 37% of the navy budget, with 18% for training and 30% for personnel. The function of the naval program was to support the national shipbuilding yards which had been hard hit by the crisis of 1929. The four battleships of the *Cavour* and *Duilio* type were improved and construction of two others was begun. Italian naval policy was conditioned however by the deliberations of the 1921 Washington conference which established precise limits for the naval armaments of the great powers.

In the war of 1915-18 there were two different air force organizations: one was army and the other navy.

The Regia Aeronautica was constituted on March 28, 1923, but the minister of the Navy refused to cede his aerial organization to the new armed force.

In the period between the two wars, discussions went on at length as to whether to privilege the strategic use of planes en masse or to make tactical use of the aviation. Nominated air minister, Italo Balbo hoped to upgrade the air force so it could carry out autonomous military operations in line with the new doctrines.

Balbo committed himself to making the most of the Italian aeronautic industry and strengthening the prestige of the regime at home and abroad by organizing and participating in great long-distance rallies, collective cruises culminating in the trans-Atlantic flight of 1933. After seven years at the summit of the ministry, at the height of his popularity, Mussolini named him governor of Libya.

He left a fleet of 3125 planes, of which only 911 were defined as "efficient from a military point of view ".

From 1935 to 1939 the Air Force was wholeheartedly committed to the conquest of Ethiopia, in the Spanish civil war and in the occupation of Albania.

THE ITALIAN COMMITMENT IN AFRICA

During the Great War Italian occupation of Libya was limited to controlling the coastal centers. By 1929 all resistance in Tripolitania had been overcome. In Cyrenaica the resistance of the rebels led to drastic measures. In 1931 Governor Badoglio and his second in command Graziani proclaimed the total reconquest.

The Italians had been in Somalia in the last fifteen years of the nineteenth century. Between 1923 and 1928 the Italian domination of Somalia was extended up to the territories of Obbia and Migiurtinia.

Perhaps the only truly popular war Italy fought during the regime was the one in Africa of 1935-36. Mussolini's position was secure, but he felt he needed a success which would give concrete form to the expectations of the Italians. Fascist propaganda succeeded in touching all the strings of national feeling, peasants and intellectuals alike.

The time was right. Mussolini did not yet consider the German renascence dangerous, but he was aware that the breaking of European balance, caused by the rearming of Berlin, would have

LIBYA, 1930s. Italo Balbo, Governor of Libya, at the inauguration of a water-scooping machine *(Fratelli Alinari Museum of the History of Photography - Miniati archive, Florence)*

stopped France and Great Britain from opposing Italian ambitions beyond a certain limit. Consequently after the Stresa Conference of 1935 in which Italy, France and Great Britain condemned German rearmament and repeated that Austria must remain independent, Mussolini decided to intervene in Ethiopia, the only independent state on the African continent and member of the League of Nations. He did not however foresee all the political and military consequences of an Italian commitment in Africa. It broke the front of the powers that had won World War I and began the process of Italo-German reconciliation.

The Italian lineup, with 110,000 soldiers and Blackshirts, 50,000 askari (European-trained African troops), 126 aircraft and many heavy vehicles, was initially under the command of De Bono. In November command passed to Badoglio, who launched an offensive in February 1936, winning all the battles thanks also to the aviation, armored cars and obvious technological supremacy. On May 5, 1936, the Italian troops entered Addis Ababa and Mussolini could declare that the war had been won. On May 9th Victor Emmanuel III was proclaimed Emperor of

SUMMER NAVY MANEUVERS, C. 1925.
Off the prow, a plane used for maritime reconnaissance is preparing to take off.
(Historical Bureau of the Navy, Rome)

TURIN, 1928
EXPOSITION. Armed Navy train. This particular vehicle, used for antinaval and anti-aircraft fire, was used, but in a less evolved model than this, in the course of World War I on the various Italian coasts. A later model of armed train also was employed in World War II to counter the French naval action on the Ligurian coast.
The model in the photo mounts a 151/40 caliber cannon.
(Historical Bureau of the Navy, Rome)

Ethiopia. Italian losses were modest with respect to those of the Abyssinians, poorly organized and with inadequate equipment. The economic effort on the part of Italy was however to have a negative effect on rearming in the years to come.

The conquest of the African country increased the prestige of the Armed Forces and thanks to a relentless propaganda campaign convinced the Italians they were a great power. Partisan guerilla warfare continued in the following years. It was not eliminated until 1941 when the English restored the throne of Ethiopia to the Emperor Haile Selassie.

THE INTERVENTION IN SPAIN

In order to broaden the area of Italian influence, speculating on the rivalry between the Germans and the French-English factions, in July 1936 Mussolini decided to intervene in Spain in aid of the generals who wanted to overthrow the Spanish republic, by formally sending "volunteers". It was important to get the jump on Germany. It was feared that Spain might enter the French orbit and the anti-communist idea had to be exploited. Catholic and bourgeois circles supported the cause of the Spanish Nationalists but the new war was never popular in Italy. The Spanish Nationalists asked for transport and fighter planes, as well as war supplies. But when the Corps of Voluntary Troops (CVT) was established, composed of 50,000 Italian soldiers, including 25,000 Blackshirts, friction with General Francisco Franco began. Hopes for turning the Spanish situation into a hegemony were ended in the battle of Guadalajara against the Republicans. Italian participation was however determining in various occasions: in Bilbao (April-June 1937), Brunete (July), in Santander (August), in Teruel, in Aragon (March-April 1938). The final success in Barcelona in January 1939 was due in great part to the CVT.

The Italian naval units were given the task of stopping supplies from reaching the ports of Republican Spain. They embarked on an intense clandestine activity, both on and under the sea, damaging the merchant ships on route to these ports.

The effort was politically of little use and harmful on the military level. The Italian motorization program found itself minus the 6,800 modern vehicles sold to Spain, 1400 pieces of artillery and 760 planes.

Nor did the Italians learn anything useful from a military point of view. They never understood how essential tactical aerial-land collaboration was.

ALBANIA

In 1915 Albania was occupied by the Italian and French troops. In the 1920s and 1930s Italy gradually increased its influence on Tirana. Various coincidences smoothed the way and led to the hypothesis of a direct occupation of the country, supported by the foreign minister Galeazzo Ciano who proposed to counterbalance the German occupation of Austria, Sudetenland, Prague, Bohemia and Moravia.

Between April 6th and 7th, 1939, thirty thousand men, with the support of the Navy and the Air Force, landed in the ports of Durazzo and Valona. Albanian reactions were weak and on April 10th the Italians had reached the borders with Yugoslavia and Greece. Victor Emmanuel III of Savoy, King of Italy, could add the title of King of Albania to that of Emperor of Ethiopia.

THE AMBIGUITIES OF MUSSOLINI'S POLICIES

Up to 1936 Italian armaments were not inferior to those of the other great States. Military involvement in Ethiopia and Spain postponed rearming while Germany was intent on rearming and France did likewise in answer.. There were problems and difficulties everywhere, but while in the other countries the economic-industrial apparatus was capable of correcting errors and making up for lost time, in Italy immobility and errors determined deficiencies about which nothing more could be done.

In October 1936 the friendship pact with Germany, the Rome-Berlin Axis, was signed. It became increasingly binding, forcing Mussolini to accept all of Hitler's initiatives up to the signing of the military alliance known as the *Pact of Steel* in May 1939, which bound the destiny of Italy to that of Germany.

Badoglio, a convinced supporter of an exclusively defensive strategy, was not even consulted.

"Mussolini of the period August 1939 to June 1940 was a 'frightened' Mussolini because he had been caught unprepared by the sudden change in the European balance provoked by his ally; stressed by the effort not to remain cut off by the decisions and events which determined them; attempting to take as few risks as possible in capturing an occasion that would never again present itself". This is how Minniti described the Duce in the months that marked the fate of Fascism.

Mussolini, who was to earn his wings as Military Pilot, prepares to take off. In the background wearing a leather pilot's helmet is Arturo Ferrarin, officer pilot of the Air Force known for his participation in 1920 in the Rome-Tokyo long-distance rally with a SVA 9.
(Air Force General Staff – Audiovisual production center, Rome)

S. 55 X hydroplanes
lined up on the seaplane
base of Orbetello. These
planes were the
protagonists of the
many transcontinental
flights undertaken in the
1920s and 1930s.
*(Air Force General Staff
– Audiovisual production
center, Rome)*

TRANS - ATLANTIC ROME - CHICAGO FLIGHT OF 1933. Italo Balbo's S. 55 X on their way to North America flying over Lisbon.
(Air Force General Staff – Audiovisual production center, Rome)

Trans - Atlantic Rome - Chicago flight of 1933. An S. 55 X seaplane riding anchor on Lake Michigan. In the background, a view of Chicago.
(Air Force General Staff – Audiovisual production center, Rome)

***TRANS - ATLANTIC
ROME - CHICAGO FLIGHT
OF 1933.*** A formation of
S.55X in flight over New
York City. (*Air Force
General Staff –
Audiovisual production
center, Rome*)

preceding page:
TRANS - ATLANTIC ROME - CHICAGO FLIGHT OF 1933. The people of New York joyously welcoming the transatlantic pilots. *(Air Force General Staff – Audiovisual production center, Rome)*

TRANS - ATLANTIC ROME - CHICAGO FLIGHT OF 1933. Arrival at Ostia of the S. 55 X at the end of the North Atlantic crossing. *(Air Force General Staff – Audiovisual production center, Rome)*

above:
Arab prisoners detained and controlled by Royal Army personnel.
(Historical Bureau of the Navy, Rome)

Local population of the Italian colonies. Presumably Italian East Africa.
(Historical Bureau of the Navy, Rome)

*NAPLES, DECEMBER
1935.* The fuselage of
a Savoia S. 81 is towed
through the streets of
Naples towards the port
where it will be
embarked for Eritrea to
be used in the Ethiopian
war.
*(Air Force General Staff
– Audiovisual production
center, Rome)*

NAPLES, DECEMBER
1935. Savoia S. 81 and
trimotor Caproni Ca.
133 ready for
embarkation.
(Air Force General Staff
– Audiovisual production
center, Rome)

following page:
ITALO-ETHIOPIAN WAR,
1935-36.
Troops embarked on the
'Gange' heading for East
Africa.
(Historical Bureau
of the Army General
Staff, Rome)

ITALO-ETHIOPIAN WAR, 1935-36. 'Caproni 101' bomber flying over the plateaus. The Ca 101 aircraft, affectionately called 'La Caprona' ('The big goat') by the crew, was extremely useful in operations in support of the troops, with bombing and reconnaissance flights, and above all bringing in fresh provisions. On the whole the use of aviation in operative, reconnaissance and logistic transportation missions was of fundamental importance for Badoglio's victory.
(Historical Bureau of the Army General Staff, Rome)

following page:
ETHIOPIAN WAR, 1935-36. Aerial photo of operations during battle.
(Air Force General Staff – Audiovisual production center, Rome)

***ITALO-ETHIOPIAN WAR,
1935-36.*** Column
marching on Addis
Ababa. The harsh terrain
and the absence of
roads sorely tried the
Italian logistic
organization.
The vehicle in the
foreground is a Pavesi
artillery tractor.
*(Historical Bureau
of the Army General
Staff, Rome)*

***ITALO-ETHIOPIAN WAR,
1935-36.*** The 14th
bomber squadron
'La Disperata' deployed
in the Airport
of Asmara. The plane is
a Caproni CA 101D/2".
*(Air Force General Staff
– Audiovisual production
center, Rome)*

Previous page, above:
TARANTO, 1936, PHOTO PRIORE. First Naval Squadron at the wharf.
(Fratelli Alinari Museum of the History of Photography – Miniati Archives, Florence)

ITALO-ETHIOPIAN WAR, 1935-1936.
Troops entering Macallé (Bersaglieri and 13th Infantry); view of the town.
(Historical Bureau of the Army General Staff, Rome)

above:
NAPLES, 1938.
Partial view of a group of Italian submarines at the San Vincenzo wharf in Naples, on the occasion of Hitler's visit to Italy.
(Historical Bureau of the Navy, Rome)

NAVAL MANOEUVERS, 1939, PHOTO BY BRUNO MINIATI.
'Zara' class heavy cruisers. Note the RO 37 reconnaissance aircraft ready to be catapulted. The camouflage is pre-war, with a red and white stripe.
(Fratelli Alinari Museum of the History of Photography – Miniati Archives, Florence)

page 76:
SPANISH CIVIL WAR, 1936-39. IMAM Ro. 37bis aircraft of the Aviazione Legionaria.
(Air Force General Staff – Audiovisual production center, Rome)

above:
**SPANISH CIVIL WAR,
MARCH 1937.**
Guadalajara – Road to
France. 100/17 – mod.
14 howitzer hidden in
the bushes.
*(Historical Bureau
of the Army General
Staff, Rome)*

**SPANISH CIVIL WAR.
PHOTO ISTITUTO LUCE.**
Barcelona. Military
parade after the
surrender of the
Republicans.
*(Historical Bureau
of the Army General
Staff, Rome)*

SPANISH CIVIL WAR,
1936-39. S. 79 'Falchi
delle Baleari' aircraft in
formation flight over the
city of Valencia
(Air Force General Staff
– Audiovisual production
center, Rome)

***Spanish Civil War,
1936-39.*** Squadron
of Fiat CR 32 fighters
in the skies over Spain.
*(Air Force General Staff
– Audiovisual production
center, Rome)*

preceding page, above:
**SPANISH CIVIL WAR,
MAY 12, 1939.** Airport
of Barajas (Madrid).
Line-up of aircraft of the
Aviazione Legionaria.
*(Air Force General Staff
– Audiovisual production
center, Rome)*

below:
**SPANISH CIVIL WAR,
1936-39.**
Trimotor S. 79 craft of
the Aviazione Legionaria
flying the skies of Spain.
This aircraft was used in
the course of the
Spanish War essentially
as a bomber, while in
World War II it became
famous as a torpedo
plane.
*(Air Force General Staff
– Audiovisual production
center, Rome)*

1939. ALBANIA. Aspects
of the daily life of the
local population during
the period of Italian
occupation.
*(Historical Bureau of the
Navy, Rome)*

World War II

On September 1, 1939, Germany invaded Poland and began World War II, without consulting Italy to whom at least four years of peace had been guaranteed. Mussolini could not disassociate himself and preferred to declare himself ready as long as the Germans furnished the materials required to complete military preparations. The Italian requests were so exorbitant that Germany could not fulfill them.

The Council of Ministers declared that Italy would not take part in military operations. This "non-belligerence" however looked very much like a simple dilatory action. In the meeting on March 18th at the Brenner, Mussolini promised Hitler he would intervene. The German offer of military collaboration was refused because Mussolini and the Armed Forces hoped to keep Germany away from the Mediterranean and had no desire to agree on a common strategy.

What Mussolini wanted was a "parallel war" to Germany's war in an attempt to solve the problem of the "freedom of the seas" and the "window on the ocean" but he thought the beginning of hostilities could be delayed.

The Armed Forces prepared to intervene doing what they could to establish its defensive nature. Badoglio on April 4th had warned Mussolini that it would take at least three years to strengthen the Italian Armed Forces.

After the beginning of the victorious German offensive in France, Mussolini, convinced that the war was about to end, concluded that Italy could lose no time in intervening. Paradoxically, "the passage from a war that was only declared to one that was effectively being fought was an unexpected necessity".

Albeit reluctantly, the King turned over "command of the troops on all fronts" to the Duce.

The Italian head of state knew that the Armed Forces were unprepared, but nevertheless he hoped for a few concrete successes, convinced that the war was about to end. The army was requested to launch a general attack. The war on the western front which broke out on June 10th and ended on June 25th involved the troops of the Western Armed Group (Gruppo Armato Ovest) and it immediately became clear that with an improvised plan of this sort the army was inefficient, prepared for defence, but not for attack. The Air Force was even asked to bomb fortified targets in mountains that were difficult to find. The battle was interrupted by the armistice signed by France.

In the first half of June, a series of incursions on military targets in Malta, considered indefensible by the English admiralty, were carried out by the 2° Aerial Squadron. Subsequently Italian planes were sent over objectives in French northern Africa to force France to ask for an armistice. This facilitated the gradual strengthening of Malta, which became a decisive element in operations in the Mediterranean.

In Northern Africa the English took the initiative with raids into the hinterland of Cyrenaica with light armored cars. On June 12th and 14th they wiped out the garrisons of Sidi Omar and the redoubt Maddalena. On June 14th they had arrived near Bardia, on the 16th the Air Force destroyed a convoy of trucks on Via Balbia. This initial contact had revealed the insufficiency of the armor plating of the Italian light tanks with respect to the perforating power of the shells of the English tanks.

WORLD WAR II. Russian front. Fiat BR20 aircraft. The below zero temperatures of the Russian winter make it necessary to preheat the oil before starting the motors. *(Air Force General Staff – Audiovisual production center, Rome)*

*WORLD WAR II, JUNE
1940.* Western front.
Saint Louis Bridge.
Operations against
France. Deployment of
pack animal divisions.
*(Historical Bureau
of the Army General
Staff, Rome)*

For political reasons, the government ordered an attack in Egyptian territory. The troops passed the Libyan-Egyptian border on September 13th, moving on Sidi el Barrani before completing their logistic preparation. On September 16th Sidi el Barrani was occupied, but the English counteroffensive on December 9th, carried out on land, sea and air, forced the Italians to retreat after have defended Bardia, Tobruk, the Cyrenaic Gebel to no avail. The last battle was fought on February 5th and 6th, south of Benghazi which was evacuated while the British were advancing towards the frontiers of Tripolitania.

A new theater of operations in Greece was opened on October 28, 1940, once more with an improvised decision and plan. The Greco-Albanian front absorbed a large number of men and means and the Navy and the Air Force found themselves involved in an extenuating operative and logistic effort.

After a few days of advance in Epirus, the Greeks counterattacked the Italian left wing and forced them to withdraw ever deeper into Albania. By the end of November Korçë and Gjirokastër had been lost, while Vlarë was threatened. In the winter of 1940-41 the bombers were attempting to stop the Greek offensive in the mountains of Albania.

Badoglio resigned, with world-wide repercussions, and the feeling that in Italy part of the establishment was keeping its distance from the regime.

The Italian counteroffensive began in March. On April 6th, the German troops arrived, penetrating Greek territory and forcing Greece to ask for an armistice.

The campaign cost the Italian army 13,755 fallen, 50,874 wounded, 12,368 with frostbite. Eleven colonels fell in the field.

In April of 1941 the German armed forces also penetrated Yugoslavia, together with the Hungarians and the Italians who reached Lubiana, occupied northern Dalmatia and established contact with the forces from Albania in Ragusa. The Air Force eliminated the Yugoslavian air forces.

The arrival of the Germans lent new vigor to operations in Northern Africa. In March 1941 Rommel attacked the British forces, reaching Benghazi and Darnah (Derna) and attacking Tobruk. The British Army counterattacked on June 15th, but was thrown back and the battle, known as the battle of Sollum, ended on the 17th with the decisive defeat of the English.

On the other hand, the situation came to a head in Eastern Africa where the Italian army had 255,000 men, but few transportation vehicles and little combat equipment. Once the war was begun, operations were carried out to occupy important sites beyond the frontier, including Kassala. The British attack came to a head in January 1941. The principal clash took place in Keren between February and March and ended with the English occupation of Asmara and Massawa.

In Somalia the troops were ranged along a 500 kilometer front, on the middle and lower Jubba River. The British forces attacked on the lower Jubba in January 1941. On February 26th they occupied Mogadishu.

Subsequently, having moved into Ethiopia, on April 6th they entered Addis Ababa. The Italians attempted to stop the English forces from uniting but the battle "of Comboleia" was a new defeat. On May 1st, the viceroy Amedeo d'Aosta arrived in Amba Alaji, where a last stand had been organized. The British forces attacked from the north and from the south, pushing ahead hordes of rebels and providing artillery support on the ground as well as in the air. On May 19, 1941 the surrender was signed while the British forces were being reunited.

left:
WORLD WAR II.
"Il popolo d'Italia",
June 10, 1940.

WORLD WAR II. African front. Cyrenaica-Tripolitania. Italian soldiers resting at the front.
(Historical Bureau of the Navy, Rome)

The forces operating in Galla Sidama and around Gondar remained armed. The former ceased resistance on July 7, 1941 and the latter on November 28th, lowering the last Italian flag to wave over Eastern Africa where 5,211 Italian soldiers died and 7,000 were wounded. The losses suffered by the colonial divisions is not known.

In the summer of 1941 Germany invaded the Soviet Union. Despite the opposition of the military summits, Mussolini decided that the Italian troops were also to participate in that campaign. Once more the German initiative conditioned Mussolini's programs.

In mid August the Italian Expeditionary Force in Russia (CSIR or Corpo di Spedizione Italiano in Russia) took part, with the division *Pasubio*, in the "Battle of the two Rivers" which wiped out the Soviet forces caught between the Dniestr and Bug rivers. On September 6th the CSIR assumed responsibility for a sector of the Dnieper and at the end of September carried out an action of encirclement, culminating in Petrikovka. In the month of October, incorporated into the German 1st Armored Force, the CSIR conquered the Donez basin with its coalfields and then occupied Gorlovka and Nikitovka.

At the end of November 1941 the Russians succeeded in stopping the German advance, initiating a great winter offensive along the entire front, from the Sea of Azov to the Gulf of Finland, which the Italians helped to hold.

At the beginning of summer 1942, the ARMIR advanced up to the Don, over a front of 270 kilometers covering the Germans on their way to Stalingrad. The north wing of the formation consisted of the three divisions of the Alpine Armed Forces.

Between August 20 and September 1, 1942 the first defensive battle on the Don took place. Between November 19 and 23, 1942, a powerful Soviet offensive succeeded in separating the German 6th Army from its supply lines, isolating it and forcing it to dwindle out around Stalingrad. The second defensive battle of the Don began at dawn on December 11th. It lasted until the 17th when the Soviet units broke through the Italian front and made deep inroads towards the logistic supply lines of the railroad. The Russian advance was momentarily con-

tained, but on January 14, 1943 the Russians began a great new offensive which forced the Italian troops to withdraw, opening the way with a series of bitter battles and massacring marches. Repatriation took place in May of 1943. There were enormous losses. Recent studies indicate that there were 90,000 fallen and missing and 43,282 wounded and frozen: more than half of those who had been sent.

Between summer and autumn of 1941 men and materials were brought into Northern Africa. In November the Italo-German Forces were ready to reconquer the stronghold of Tobruk. Fighting with the English forces continued until December when Rommel decided to withdraw, evacuating Cyrenaica. Between December and January two convoys transporting tanks, munitions, fuel managed to reach Tripoli. Rommel then attacked on January 21, 1942, forcing the enemy to withdraw. On January 29th Benghazi was reoccupied. In fifteen days Cyrenaica had been reconquered. On May 26th the offensive of the Italo-German Forces began with the battle known as Ain el Gazala. On June 20th Tobruk was reached. The English withdrew to Egypt with the Germans and the Italians hot on their heels. Between July and October three battles were fought at El Alamein, with an ever weaker Italo-German army and a much stronger British force. On October 24, 1942, when the English launched the third Battle of el-Alamein, the fate of Northern Africa had been decided, for the Anglo-American Expedition Corps was about to land in Morocco. The Italo-German Forces held out for ten days. Then Rommel decided to retreat in haste, taking most of the German troops to safety, but leaving the Italian units who had no means of transportation behind. Rommel withdrew to Tunisia and, at the end of December, the Italian staff evacuated Tripolitania. The forces of the Axis, lined up in Tunisia against the British 8th Army, were known as the 1st Army and General Messe was put in command. He succeeded in keeping together units demoralized by a long retreat and gave them the wherewithal to achieve a defensive victory on the Mareth line and to accom-

WORLD WAR II. Italian soldiers boarding an S. 81 aircraft. During the war the Royal Air Force (Regia Aeronautica) saw to the transport of troops and materials to almost all the operational theaters. The "Servizi Aerei Speciali" was created and its men went on particularly dangerous missions and the losses were considerable. *(Air Force General Staff – Audiovisual production center, Rome)*

plish the difficult withdrawal up to Enfidaville. In this position he resisted repeated attacks, up until the final surrender, which was authorized by Rome when the German troops had already surrendered. The 1st Army, resisting up to May 13th, the last of the German-Italian units, concluded the North African campaign with honor. It had cost the Italian army 20,765 fallen, 7,624 wounded and 17,058 missing.

The principal commitments of the Navy in the Mediterranean can be summed up in two specific tasks:

• maintaining communications between the lands across the seas (Libya, Albania, Greece, Dodecanese) to support the activities of the fighting land forces;

• foiling the movements of the adversaries in support of the base of Malta.

The former, commonly known as the "battle of the convoys", was carried out with a spirit of sacrifice by the men of the Navy and Merchant Marine, despite the lack of convoy aircraft carriers and coordination with the Air Forces. The second objective led to naval encounters with the English naval air forces in the Mediterranean.

WORLD WAR II, 1941.
East Africa. The Italian
troops under the orders
of the Duke of Aosta
leaving the fortress of
Amba Alagi. The English
are presenting arms.
*(Historical Bureau of the
General Headquarters of
the Carabinieri Corps,
Rome)*

The first encounter took place on July 10, 1940 when the Italian navy, under the command of Admiral Campioni, who had completed his mission of escorting a convoy to Benghazi, encountered the Mediterranean Fleet, on its way from Malta to Alexandria (Egypt), at Punta Stilo. The battle lasted three hours and ended in a draw. In the meanwhile the Italian bombers kept the English navy in shooting range throughout the day without appreciable results.

On November 12th an English air raid struck the Italian fleet, concentrated in the port of Taranto, and the battleships *Cavour, Littorio, Duilio* were put out of action.

After this success, the English admiral decided to send a merchant convoy to Malta via Gibraltar, without rounding Africa. The battle of Cape Teulada, on November 27th, was over after a few minutes fire. The English succeeded in having their convoys arrive in Malta and

Alexandria and in getting other units out of the Mediterranean despite the fact that the Navy had the task of keeping the English from joining the two Mediterranean fleets from Alexandria and Gibraltar in Malta.

On February 9, 1941, an English fleet left Gibraltar and bombarded the port of Genoa: 32 ships were hit with light damage. Greater damage was inflicted on the factories and civilian buildings with 144 dead and 272 wounded. On account of poor interpretation of the sightings (a French convoy was passing through the area) and incomplete coordination, the Italian units departing from La Spezia were unable to intercept the English ships and they left undisturbed.

At the end of March the Navy decided to attack the English who were strengthening the Greek front. At Gaudo, Admiral Iachino attacked an enemy already informed of the Italian intentions. On his way back to Italy torpedo bombers attacked the Italian warship *Vittorio Veneto* and the cruiser *Pola* southwest of Cape Matapàn in southern Greece.

It was only with the aid of the Germans that the Italian navy succeeded in inflicting losses on the English convoys and escort ships in the course of 1942. The losses sustained by the English and the forces of the Axis were considerable in the battle known as "mid June". But it was a great tactical victory for the Axis. The "battle of mid August" was the most important of all the aeronaval battles in the Mediterranean. The Axis forces employed imposing means, some of which were used for the first time.

While the naval encounters were not always successful, the actions by the surface and sub assault means (MTM / MTS / motoroboats and SLIC known as "pigs" and pocket smg) and the "gamma" swimmers in the ports of Gibraltar - Algeciras, Alexandria, Suda, Algiers, Alexandretta - were much more satisfying. The men of the X Flotilla MAS seriously damaged the warships *Valiant* and *Queen Elisabeth*, sinking the cruiser *York* and other military units up to 7,200 tons and almost twice as many merchant marine ships, meriting 29 gold medals, 104 silver medals and 33 bronze medals.

The sacrifice of the sub components was high: the submarines deployed in the Mediterranean, Red Sea, Indian Ocean, in the Atlantic (the base is known as Betasom) carried out 6341 missions sinking 128 merchant ships and 17 military units for 673,212 tons, but 86 ships never returned to base.

Mussolini had great faith in the capacities of the Air Force to which he entrusted the role of "global force". When Italy entered the war, it had 3000 aircraft, of which only 1796 were efficient and ready for use. They were moreover scattered over a vast checkerboard. Almost the entire Air Force was involved in furnishing air support to the land and sea forces, in the Alps, in northern Africa, in the Mediterranean, Greece, eastern Africa, Russia, Tunisia, Sicily.

The Italian Air Corps (Corpo Aereo Italiano CAI) however did not do well and upon request of the Germans was withdrawn from the English Channel where the Italian planes were unable to keep up with the Luftwaffe.

In Italian East Africa the only concrete continuing contacts were ensured by the transportation sectors of the Air Force. In Libya the Air Force was employed in trying to halt the in-depth penetration of the British motorized commandos. Lastly the resistance of the Italian troops in Tunisia was made possible by the massive use of hundreds of trucks which decimated men and equipment.

In the Mediterranean, the Axis forces were constantly active and the torpedo plane divisions were in full force against the British convoys. An example is the torpedoing of the battleship *Nelson* on September 27, 1941.

FROM THE FALL OF FASCISM TO THE ARMISTICE

One of the consequences of the loss of Northern Africa was the invasion of the metropolitan territory by the Anglo-American forces. The landing in Sicily, prepared some time earlier, was the first large amphibious operation of World War II. The Anglo-Americans attacked between July 9th and 10th, 1943, landing infantry, artillery, tanks along 150 kilometers of coast, preceded by parachute launches between Siracusa and Gela. The Italian coastal units, insufficiently armed and lacking support in the form of permanent fortifications, were unable to halt the allied war machine. The counterattack was stopped by the fire of the naval artillery. The air forces deployed in Sicily and Sardinia were decimated in dogfights and field incursions.

The fall of the Fascist government, Mussolini's resignation on July 25th, his arrest and the creation of Badoglio's government were the consequence of the military defeats and an ungluing between the regime and the populace which had become evident in that year. Malcontent was rife and also came to a head in general strikes in the factories in the north.

Fascism had come to an end, but not the Fascist war. On the evening of July 25th Badoglio said on the radio"the war goes on".

In Sicily on the evening of July 27th, General Hube, who had all the German troops under his command, received orders to retreat and evacuate the island, transferring all the forces to the continent.

The Italians remained alone and after hard fighting (4,678 soldiers fell) finished evacuating the island at dawn of August 17th.

After a few isolated attempts which had no outcome, including diplomatic efforts, the commander in chief General Ambrosio, supported by the Head of the Government Badoglio and with the assent of the King, sent General Castellano to Spain and Portugal to discuss an armistice with the Allies.

Negotiations were concluded on September 3rd while the Allies were landing in Reggio Calabria and in Salerno and Taranto on September 9th.

The announcement of the armistice, conceded by the Allies, was broadcast on the radio the evening of September 8, 1943, catching the Italian soldiers scattered throughout the world unprepared and left without orders and information. The G.U. Headquarters subordinated to the SMRE had received the Memoria O.P. 44 which furnished instructions on conduct regarding the Germans in case of an armistice, but it was not followed up by the necessary documents. These were moments of great confusion, aggravated by political and military summits. The morning of September 9th the King Victor Emmanuel III and Badoglio, the head of the government, abandoned Rome and sought refuge in Brindisi, occupied by the allies.

A long and tragic period of total confusion followed both at home and abroad for civilians and military alike.

In Italy, Sicily and Calabria were occupied by the Anglo-Americans. The rest of the peninsula was occupied and controlled by the Germans who, after July 25th, had stationed their forces so they could control all vital points, the liaison headquarters, railroads, bridges, the most important highway junctions and encapsulate the Italian forces.

Orders were clear: arrest and deport Italian soldiers who had become enemies. There were many, too many soldiers and disarmed officers sent to the work camps in Germany. The Germans applied the orders received wherever there were Italians: in Provence, Slovenia, Croatia, Dalmatia, Herzegovina, Montenegro, Albania, Greece, the Aegean and the Far East.

The detachments stationed throughout Italy were in the worst conditions to maintain a valid resistance for on the whole they lacked mobility and were scattered here and there along the coast or occupied in tasks of a territorial nature which led to the scattering of men and means over vast areas.

There was one particular clause in the armistice which concerned the naval units. They were principally stationed in the ports of Taranto, La Spezia, Genoa, Pola. The units which left Taranto had no trouble in reaching Malta. The naval battle squadron, under the command of Admiral Bergamini, and other units, left La Spezia and Genoa and headed for Sardinia. On the way the fleet was attacked by German planes. The battleship *Roma* was hit and sank with Bergamini and 1352 men. When the attack ended the units, under the command of Admiral Oliva, headed for the allied port of Bona.

Many of the Air Force pilots headed for the airports in southern Italy.

The Italian planes were prevalently employed outside Italy in offensives against the Germans and in defensive operations in favor of the Italian and Allied contingents in the Balkans and the Ionian islands. The Italian Air Force fought side by side with the Anglo-Americans using only their own planes up to the middle of September 1944 when the Allies turned over aircraft to them and strengthened the Italian Air Force divisions.

WORLD WAR II. Balkan front. Italian infantry at Sussak returning from a mopping-up operation *(Historical Bureau of the Army General Staff, Rome)*

WORLD WAR II, JULY 10, 1940. The naval battle of Punta Stilo. Photo taken from battleship 'Cavour' during exchange of artillery fire with the English naval units. *(Historical Bureau of the Army General Staff, Rome)*

left:
WORLD WAR II. Navy personnel destined for aerial surveillance in Massaua. In the foreground the aereophones, acoustic equipment which amplified the sound of approaching aircraft. Also visible are Breda 13.2 mm machine guns, with the members of the arms crew.
(Historical Bureau of the Navy, Rome)

WORLD WAR II.
Northern Africa. Italian anti-aircraft battery in action. *(Air Force General Staff – Audiovisual production center, Rome)*

preceding page, above:
WORLD WAR II.
African front, firing practice of the zaptié divisions of the empire. The soldiers shoulder Breda Mod. 30 caliber 6.5 mm. machine guns.
(Historical Bureau of the General Headquarters of the Carabinieri Corps, Rome)

WORLD WAR II. African front. The members of the I Company of the I Gruppo Carabinieri mobilized who lost their lives at Culqualbert on Nov. 21, 1941. The photo was taken a month before that date.
(Historical Bureau of the General Headquarters of the Carabinieri Corps, Rome)

WORLD WAR II.
Northern Africa. Construction of a gun shield for a Fiat CR 42 fighter plane.
(Historical Bureau of the Army General Staff, Rome)

right:
WORLD WAR II.
Northern Africa. Sappers of the 'Centauro' division cutting a passage through a barbed wire barrier.
(Historical Bureau of the Army General Staff, Rome)

WORLD WAR II.
Northern Africa. Squads of Bersaglieri stationed in the Cyrenaic Gebel. The soldier in the foreground shoulders a BREN machine gun rifle taken from the English.
(Historical Bureau of the Army General Staff, Rome)

WORLD WAR II. African front. San Marco Battalion divisions, Tobruk. They are armed with automatic Beretta mod. 38/A muskets *(Historical Bureau of the Navy, Rome)*

World War II. Russian
front. Building an ice
shelter for lodging
the troops.
*(Historical Bureau
of the Army General
Staff, Rome)*

World War II. Russian front. C.S.I.R. (Italian Expeditionary Corps in Russia) soldiers are stringing telephone lines *(Historical Bureau of the Army General Staff, Rome)*

World War II, July 3, 1941. The Duce reviewing the Torino Division in Rome before the departure for Russia. *(Historical Bureau of the Army General Staff, Rome)*

WORLD WAR II. Russian front. The divisions of the IInd Army Corps going through the city of Nowo Moskowsk. *(HHistorical Bureau of the General Headquarters of the Carabinieri Corps, Rome)*

WORLD WAR II.
Greek-Albanian front:
pier built by the military
engineers.
*(Historical Bureau
of the Army General
Staff, Rome)*

WORLD WAR II, APRIL 13, 1941. Yugoslavian front. Valle Ostreni: troops on the march. *(Historical Bureau of the General Headquarters of the Carabinieri Corps, Rome)*

WORLD WAR II. SM 79
aircraft on a bombing
flight on Malta.
*(Air Force General Staff
– Audiovisual production
center, Rome)*

TRIESTE, 1942.
The camouflaged
battleship 'Roma' lying
at anchor in the port of
Trieste.
*(Historical Bureau of the
Navy, Rome)*

World War II,
October 24, 1941.
Central Mediterranean:
the English steamship
"Empire Guillemot"
sinking after being hit by
a torpedo launched by
an SM.79 of the 283rd
Squadron.
(Air Force General Staff
– Audiovisual production
center, Rome)

WORLD WAR II, JUNE 5, 1943. Bombing of the Italian naval squad in the port of La Spezia by American heavy bombers.
(Historical Bureau of the Navy, Rome)

The Contribution of the Armed Forces to the War of Liberation

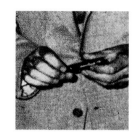

n the face of a lack of orders and the ensuing disorientation, after the Armistice was announced everything imaginable happened in the Armed Forces. As General Bovio wrote "The sudden and almost total dissolution of the army in the tragic days of September 1943 can only be correctly understood and evaluated by accepting reality, realizing that in that moment the army, worn out in its means and morale by three years of unsuccessful war, was a great body but without a soul, a great accumulation of badly nourished men, poorly equipped, poorly armed, rather badly organized". Many of the Corps and divisions were dissolved by the commanders themselves to save the men from being captured, others surrendered without fighting, still others disbanded. There were however also detachments which held out against German attacks with episodic and isolated fighting.

Abroad, armed reactions, resistance and real battles against the Germans took place in Provence, Corsica, Dalmatia, Yugoslavia, Albania, Thessaly, in the Ionian islands and in the islands of the Aegean. The resistance of the *Acqui* division in Cefalonia, which ended with a ferocious German reprisal, is symbolic. Of 11,500 men, over 9,000 either died fighting, were shot or lost at sea.

A few large units to flank the allied Armed Forces could have been organized in southern Italy but the victors were reluctant to accept Italian contingents. The only exception were the Carabinieri whose action in the Kingdom of the south was unanimously judged by the allied forces as an element of stability as early as 1943.

The 1st Motorized Group (I Raggruppamento Motorizzato) was established on September 27th in the Leccese and was in action from December 1943 to April 1944, fighting at Monte Lungo (December 1943) and Monte Marrone (March 1944). On October 16th Italy obtained co-belligerance with the Allies, after declaring war on Germany. On April 17, 1944 the Group was officially called the Italian Liberation Corps (Corpo Italiano di Liberazione CIL) and participated in a series of operations along the Adriatic, occupying L'Aquila, Teramo, Macerata, Jesi, Urbino.

The contribution of the Italian units to the Anglo-American war operations in Italy constituted one of the events which effectively began the reconstruction of the nation.

The Bonomi government energetically promoted broadening Italian participation in the war and was granted the right to prepare six divisions to use in the front lines, called the "Combat Groups". Officers and soldiers of these units fought with English arms and equipment on the Adriatic side. The *Cremona* Group was the first to enter Venice, the *Friuli* Group liberated Bologna, on April 21st, together with the *Legnano* Group. The *Folgore* Combat Group, formed of paratroopers of the *Nembo* Regiment and sailors of the *S. Marco* fought hard along the Monte Castellazzo-Cadriano ridge. Another 200,000 Italian soldiers were used by the Allies as "auxiliary units" on the front as well as in the hinterland.

The postwar Italian army was created around these Groups.

Mention must also be made, together with the men who fought in Italy, of the Italian *Garibaldi* Division which fought in Yugoslavia, from 1943 to 1945, as part of the Yugoslavian Popular Liberating Army.

The Navy cooperated with the Allies with units of all types to escort convoys, hydrographic surveys and special missions for the recovery of information in the Adriatic, transportation of personnel and materials, training of the aeronaval forces. There were 20 thousand missions cov-

CASSIBILE (SICILY), SEPT. 3, 1943. General Castellano as Badoglio's delegate signs the armistice. *(Historical Bureau of the Army General Staff, Rome)*

VICTOR EMMANUEL III, KING OF ITALY (1900-1946). PHOTO FRATELLI ALINARI.
(Alinari Archives – Alinari archive, Florence)

PIETRO BADOGLIO, FIELD MARSHAL OF ITALY, HEAD OF THE GOVERNMENT FROM JULY 26, 1943 TO JUNE 6, 1944. PHOTO FRATELLI ALINARI.
(Alinari Archives – Alinari archive, Florence)

ROME 1945-46.
Assistance to veterans.
Missing persons
information center.
To be noted on the wall
the photographs of
soldiers the families
are looking for.
*(Historical Bureau
of the Army General
Staff, Rome)*

ering almost three million miles. The Resistance began in Italy the evening of September 8th, principally by officers and soldiers who had escaped disarmament and capture. They were joined by civilian volunteers of all ages and social conditions.

In Rome the Fronte Clandestino Militare della Resistenza took in and organized above all army and air force personnel. Linked with the organizations of the Carabinieri and the Guardia di Finanza, it carried out operations of defensive and informative nature in the city and was active in Lazio and the Abruzzi. The 67 victims of the Fosse Ardeatine belonged to the Fronte, including Colonel Giuseppe Cordero Lanza di Montezemolo, and those shot at Forte Bravetta and La Storta.

In Val d'Aosta the Resistance was almost completely organized and directed by the military. Bands of soldiers were active in Val d'Ossola, in the Langhe, in Lombardy, the Veneto, in Friuli, in Venezia Giulia, Liguria, Emilia Romagna, Tuscany, Umbria, the Marches.

The hundreds of gold medals for military valor bear witness to the importance of what these soldiers did in the struggle for liberation. Even so, as early as 1948 General Scala lamented the fact that the contribution of the Armed Forces to the war of liberation, now fully acknowledged, was being underrated.

ITALIAN PRISONERS AND INTERNEES

Next to the Italian soldiers who took up arms with the Allies, moving up the peninsula from the south, and the thousands of officers who organized the resistance against the Germans in the mountains, the sacrifice and testimony given by soldiers of all ranks and files interned in the concentration camps in Germany and Poland must not be forgotten. Captured in a moment of general disorientation or after unfortunate battles, over 800,000 non-commissioned men and soldiers and 14,033 officers were interned in the German concentration camps. Considered "interned" rather than prisoners of war so they could not claim the application of juridical guarantees, they stoically faced humiliating conditions of life and refused to join the German army and then that of the Republic of Salò.

Of the interned soldiers 98.7% chose hunger, cold, deprivation and death, but refused to return to Italy to fight their own people.

About forty thousand interned soldiers died as a result of the deprivations, hardships, tuberculosis, maltreatment. Many were shot because they were suspected of acts of sabotage in the industrial centers or mines where they were forced to work.

***WAR OF LIBERATION,
ROME, SEPTEMBER
1943.*** Italian infantry
troops supported by
armored troops in the
fighting at Porta San
Paolo. In the
background a self-
propelled 75. mm. piece
of artillery.
*(Historical Bureau of the
General Headquarters of
the Carabinieri Corps,
Rome)*

WAR OF LIBERATION, NOVEMBER 18, 1944.
General Mark Clark awarding the decoration for merit to General Roberto Bencivenga for having organized the resistance in the zone of Rome.
(Historical Bureau of the Army General Staff, Rome)

WAR OF LIBERATION. THE
FOUR DAYS OF NAPLES
(SEPTEMBER 28 –
OCTOBER 1, 1943).
The Carabinieri Captain
Antonio Penne at the
head of the insurgents.
(Historical Bureau of the
General Headquarters of
the Carabinieri Corps,
Rome)

following page:
WAR OF LIBERATION,
FOUR DAYS OF NAPLES
(SEPTEMBER 28 –
OCTOBER 1, 1943).
Insurgents plundering
a depot of German light
arms, abandoned during
the retreat. The rifles
are German Mauser
KAR 98.
(Army General Staff –
Cine-photo television and
exhibition production
agency, Rome)

War of Liberation.
Italian soldiers who had
disbanded after
September 8, 1943,
respond to the call to
arms for the
reconstruction of the
army divisions. The I[st]
Motorized Italian Group
is constituted.
*(Historical Bureau
of the Army General
Staff, Rome)*

***WAR OF LIBERATION,
DECEMBER 9, 1943.***
The Italian infantry of
the I[st] Motorized Group
advancing among the
rocks on Monte Lungo.
*(Historical Bureau
of the Army General
Staff, Rome)*

WAR OF LIBERATION, MONTE LUNGO, DECEMBER 1943. War of Liberation. General Mark Clark, Commander of the American 5th Army, at a meeting with General Vincenzo Dapino, commander of the I[st] Motorized Group. *(Historical Bureau of the Army General Staff, Rome)*

WAR OF LIBERATION.
C.I.L. troops in war gear
passing through.
*(Historical Bureau of the
General Headquarters of
the Carabinieri Corps,
Rome)*

preceding page:
MARCH. 1944. Marshal Messe, Chief of Staff of the Royal Italian Army, passes the Bersaglieri of the 4° 'Vercelli' regiment of the C.I.L. in review. *(Historical Bureau of the General Headquarters of the Carabinieri Corps, Rome)*

WAR OF LIBERATION. The President of the Council Bonomi visiting Italian patriots in Cassino. *(Fratelli Alinari Museum of the History of Photography, Florence)*

WAR OF LIBERATION.
Italian auxiliary units
reconstructing a
destroyed bridge on the
road between Vasto and
Casalbordino.
*(Historical Bureau
of the Army General
Staff, Rome)*

WAR OF LIBERATION.
Italian emplacement
of medium mortars in
the Comacchio valleys.
*(Historical Bureau
of the Army General
Staff, Rome)*

WAR OF LIBERATION, APRIL 24, 1945. Italian soldiers of the Combat Groups around Prince Umberto during a visit to the front.
(Fratelli Alinari Museum of the History of Photography, Florence)

WAR OF LIBERATION.
Aircraft of the
Aeronautica del Sud (Air
Force of the South) on
the field in Lecce
Galatina. In the
foreground a Macchi
MC. 205 of the 155th
Group.
*(Air Force General Staff
– Audiovisual production
center, Rome)*

WAR OF LIBERATION.
After September 8th, the fasces, symbols of the fallen Fascist regime, were removed from the Italian Air Force planes and replaced by tri-color cockades.
(Air Force General Staff – Audiovisual production center, Rome)

WAR OF LIBERATION.
Supply operations for a
Macchi fighter of the co-
belligerent Air Force in
an airport in Southern
Italy. *(Air Force General
Staff – Audiovisual
production center,
Rome)*

WAR OF LIBERATION. Specialists of the Technical Fighter Service at work on a few Macchi MC. 202 planes in a hangar in the airport of Lecce Galatina. *(Air Force General Staff – Audiovisual production center, Rome)*

WAR OF LIBERATION.
MC. 205 Macchi of the
Southern Air Force. This
aircraft participated on
October 6, 1943 in a
flight over Rome during
which handbills were
launched on the city.
*(Air Force General Staff
– Audiovisual production
center, Rome)*

GERMANY 1944.
Italian soldiers, prisoners of war, waiting for the morning roll call in a Nazi lager. *(National Association of Veterans from Imprisonment and Internment, Rome)*

following page,
top to bottom:

GERMANY 1944. Italian soldiers, prisoners of war, preparing their meal from roots and grasses they have gathered.
(National Association of Veterans from Imprisonment and Internment, Rome)

WAR OF LIBERATION, 1945. Valle dell'Indice – north of Bologna. Camp in an operations zone of the 39th Section Carabinieri of the Legnano Combat Group.
(Historical Bureau of the General Headquarters of the Carabinieri Corps, Rome)

WAR OF LIBERATION. Two Carabinieri and two Bersaglieri entering Bologna in the liberation of the city. They are armed with American Thompson machine guns.
(Historical Bureau of the General Headquarters of the Carabinieri Corps, Rome)

right:
WAR OF LIBERATION, 1944. Carabinieri in Rome after the liberation of the city. *(Historical Bureau of the General Headquarters of the Carabinieri Corps, Rome)*

WAR OF LIBERATION, JUNE 4, 1944. The first Italian troops to enter Rome are welcomed by the jubilant population. *(Historical Bureau of the Army General Staff, Rome)*

GERMANY 1945.
The Allied troops freeing
prisoners of war in the
concentration camps.
*(Historical Bureau
of the Army General
Staff, Rome)*

above:

WAR OF LIBERATION, AUGUST 1944. Entry of the Allies in Florence. *(Historical Bureau of the Army General Staff, Rome)*

WAR OF LIBERATION. First page of the "Giornale dell'Aviatore", May 3, 1945, dedicated to the activity of the Italian Air Force during the war of liberation. *(Air Force General Staff – Audiovisual production center, Rome)*

following page:

THE C.I.L. PARTISANS PARADE IN MILAN, APRIL 1945. At the center is Colonel Ratti. *(Historical Bureau of the Army General Staff, Rome)*

The Armed Forces in Republican Italy

The army, which was almost completely destroyed after the armistice, salvaged a strong nucleus in the six Combat Groups, which took part in the operations for breaking through the Gothic Line and the liberation of north Italy, as part of the right wing of the allied line-up.

Three divisions for internal safety, directly dependent on the Ministry of War, were stationed in Sardinia (one) and in Sicily (two) where the separatist tendencies in need of decisive action were strong.

In the meanwhile the soldiers liberated from the German concentration camps and the prisoners of war captured before the armistice by the victorious armies were returning home.

In August 1945 the Allied Military Mission gave the first directives on the organization of the transitional army, under the two-fold control of the Italian government and the Allied Commission, which was defined between autumn 1945 and spring 1946, leading to the first postwar organic regulations. In February 1947 the new Ministry of Defense replaced the three traditional military ministries.

In February 1947, when the Paris peace treaty was signed, the transitional army had been completed.

Although Italy held the status of co-belligerent, it was treated like a defeated State and was subject to both political and economical provisions. Italy had to reduce the size of its armed forces and the possibilities of their deployment. The Army could not have more than 250,000 men, including the Carabinieri. The Navy was cut down to 25,000 men with 67,000 tons of shipping. The best units were handed over to the Allies as war reparations. The Air Force could have at most 200 armed fighter planes, another 150 unarmed aircraft and 25,000 men.

The more delicate problems arose along the eastern border, where the Yugoslavs had occupied a good part of Venezia Giulia in 1945 and also claimed Trieste. After years of tension, in 1954 Trieste was finally reunited with Italy.

The future of the Armed Forces was defined by the Constituent Assembly in five articles (11, 52, 87, 98, 103).

Article 11 says "Italy repudiates war as an instrument of offence to the liberty of other peoples and as a means for resolving international controversies; it consents, in conditions of parity with the other States, to the limitation of its sovereignty necessary for a system which ensures peace and justice among nations, promotes and favors the international organizations addressed to this purpose".

On January 1, 1948, when the Constitution became law, on all ships, all airports, all barracks the soldiers presented arms in honor of the new code of the Republic.

On June 2, 1948, on the first anniversary celebration of the Republic, the programs were centered on the acceptance of the command of the Armed Forces by the president of the Republic Luigi Einaudi.

THE SECOND POSTWAR PERIOD

The Italian economy was in disastrous conditions at the end of the war. Industrial production was a third of what it was before the war, agriculture 40%, the zootechnical patrimony was almost destroyed. Italy was in dire straits. Roads, bridges, railroads were unserviceable. Unemployment

ROME, 1945. PHOTO OSVALDO RESTALDI.
Truck serving as a city bus. *(Fratelli Alinari Museum of the History of Photography, Florence)*

was high. In the north it was hard to maintain the public order while in the south peasants and day laborers occupied the lands. The events of the years 1943-45 had broadened the fracture between the north and south of the country with its radically different experiences: Allied occupation in the south, German occupation in the north. With the reconstitution of the political parties, Italy laboriously began to move towards a parliamentary democracy.

The progressive expulsion of the left wing parties from the government after a period of anti-fascist unity, and the acceptance of the Marshall plan, directed Italy towards the western block. This choice was consolidated by the vote of April 18, 1948, with the overwhelming victory of Alcide De Gasperi's Christian Democrats. The following year the gravity of the economic situation and the social tensions, military vulnerability, bitter political struggles, were all factors which convinced De Gasperi of the expediency of adhering to the Atlantic Pact, guaranteeing a closer political and military integration with the West.

In the 1950s De Gasperi shared the ideal of a Europe united in the name of peace, democracy and economic cooperation with the German Adenauer, the English Churchill, the French Maurice Schumann, the Belgian Paul-Henri Spaak. The first concrete realization dates to 1951 with the creation of the *European Coal and Steel Community*, followed in 1957 by the Treaty of Rome which instituted the *European Economic Community* (EEC).

Even so the status of defeated nation, and the difficult economic situation lowered the pres-

tige of the Armed Forces in the second postwar period. The unhappy experience connected with Fascist patriotic and military rhetoric which had resulted in the distressing experience of World War II, for long had a negative effect on the relationship between the Armed Forces and society.

Internal political confrontations brought the communist opposition to consider the Armed Forces as a potential instrument of what they considered a hostile power, while the majority and the minority mutually contested the subaltern nature of their respective ties with foreign powers.

A fracture and an unjust isolation was created between the civilian society and the military apparatus. It provoked malaise and de-motivation in the echelons, at the same time creating an anti-military feeling, instrumental for some, deeply felt for others. For decades in Italy everything that had to do with the military met with a tenacious and diffused resistance.

The indifference which for years has surrounded the Armed Forces may also have been the consequence of an awareness of the modest international role played by Italy, added to the hostility of various movements of opinion. The scarce attention of the representative institutions and the lack of interest on the part of the media contributed to increasing the sense of separation. The first to break that isolation by opening the barracks to everyone was Giovanni Spadolini, minister of the defense.

NAPLES, 1945.
War-time distribution of bread. *(Fratelli Alinari Museum of the History of Photography, Florence)*

NAPLES, 1944-45.
Provisions arriving in the
Port of Naples.
*(Fratelli Alinari Museum
of the History of
Photography, Florence)*

ROME, JUNE 5, 1946.
The Minister of the
Interior Romita
announces the results
of the institutional
referendum.
*(Alinari Archives - TEAM
Archive, Florence)*

ROME, 1946, PHOTO
ISTITUTO LUCE. Nenni
and De Gasperi in front
of the Palazzo
Giustiniani.
*(Istituto Luce /
Management Alinari
Archives, Florence)*

ROME, DECEMBER 27, 1947. PHOTO ISTITUTO LUCE. Palazzo Giustiniani. The new Constitution is signed by the provisory Head of State Enrico De Nicola, who will then take the title of President of the Republic. *(Istituto Luce / Management Alinari Archives, Florence)*

The Armed Forces for Italy

In times of peace the Armed Forces always came to the aid of those struck by natural calamities. The list of interventions is too long and we can only mention a few of the events of the more recent decades.

THE GREAT FLOOD OF THE POLESINE

On November 14, 1951, the Po and the Adige Rivers overflowed their banks, flooding the entire Polesine and seriously damaging men and things in those areas. It was an enormous tragedy which struck a populace that was already poor.

The Armed Forces and the forces of the Police provided men and means for rescue operations, transportation and communication activities.

The highly complex organization of the interventions was made even more difficult by the prohibitive conditions of the environment and the climate.

Many homeless families found their first shelter in the barracks of Mantua, Bologna, Verona, Milan, Bolzano, Bressanone, Vicenza, Turin, Udine, Treviso.

THE DISASTER OF VAJONT

The evening of October 9, 1963 a landslide in the basin of the Vajont, in the province of Belluno, raised an enormous mass of 5 million cubic meters of water which completely destroyed the town of Longarone, and damaged some of the neighboring towns. There were 3000 victims. It took the military a month and a half to retrieve the corpses sunk in the mud. They had to be taken out one by one to keep them intact.

The Armed Forces and the forces of the Police also took over health care, furnished the civilian population with food, transported the refugees and their belongings to centers set up for the purpose, salvaged cattle that had been left unattended as well as abandoned household goods, saw to the reclamation and disinfecting of the disaster areas, repaired roads, and controlled the geological situation of the north slopes of Mount Toc, from which the landslide had detached.

THE FLOODS OF 1966

After a week of exceptionally bad weather in the northern and central regions of the peninsula, on November 4, 1966 rivers and streams overflowed their banks and flooded areas in Lombardy, Trentino Alto Adige, Veneto, Friuli, in Carnia, the Polesine, in Tuscany. Everywhere the Armed Forces came to the aid of the people.

When the Arno River broke through its banks in Florence, a wall of water six meters high swept over the city, flooding houses and palazzi, museums and libraries. When it withdrew the city was knee-high in mud.

Orders were first to save as many human lives as possible and rescue families and individuals who were homeless, without food and clothing. Thereafter, once the flood tide had passed, the principal tasks were to facilitate the outflow of the waters, empty cellars, clear the streets of the enormous mass of mud and putrid material left behind, and restore electric power. In Florence the army was also used to remove and salvage books and documents from libraries, State archives, art institutes.

POLESINE 1951.
Carabinieri helping save the victims of the flood of the Polesine. *(Historical Bureau of the General Headquarters of the Carabinieri Corps, Rome)*

The Town Council of Florence thanked the Armed Forces with a placard that was posted in the city streets.

> *FLORENTINES,*
> *On November 4th the city was preparing to celebrate, in the day of victory, the Armed Forces of the National Defense, when the furious waters of the Arno invaded the city. In no time the military of all Branches could be seen aiding the victims of the flood (…) They worked for a full month, willingly and generously, ready to do anything however repugnant, whatever service, no matter how dangerous (…) heedless of danger and with a sense of altruism, and youthful enthusiasm, led by Officers of the most humane understanding. They are now leaving, after meriting the admiration and gratefulness of the entire city. FLORENTINES,*
> *Let us, with grateful spirit, take our leave from these sons of the Italian people, these incomparable soldiers of ours, wishing for them, together with our thanks, that they may always lead a serene, generous and beneficial life.*
>
> *THE TOWN COUNCIL*

FLORENCE, 1966.
Effects of the flood on the Florentine Lungarni.
(Historical Bureau of the Navy, Rome)

THE BELICE EARTHQUAKE

The afternoon of January 14, 1968, a violent earthquake struck in the Belice valley in western Sicily. There were other shocks on the 15th and on the 25th of January, and towns were destroyed with grave damage to persons and things. The troops hastened in from Palermo, Trapani, Messina, Catania, Bari, Rome, Milan and Udine, with trucks, equipment, ambulances, camp kitchens. They worked in the various centers of the disaster area, clearing away the ruins, retrieving the dead and wounded, tearing down precarious walls, distributing food to the civilian population, setting up tent cities. The climate was harsh, the weather often bad. Hundreds of those who survived the disaster and were homeless were lodged in the barracks of Palermo and Trapani.

THE EARTHQUAKE IN FRIULI VENEZIA GIULIA

On May 6, 1976 a violent earthquake struck the provinces of Udine and Pordenone. There were 1,000 dead, 3,000 wounded, 40,000 homeless. The sectors of the Armed Forces together with the firemen and the Red Cross worked incessantly to pull persons who were still alive from the ruins, send the wounded to centers, distribute food, blankets and clothing, raise tent cities, shore up damaged buildings.

THE EARTHQUAKE IN CAMPANIA AND BASILICATA

On November 23, 1980 two quakes of the tenth degree on the Mercalli scale raised havoc in a vast area in the southern Apennines between Irpinia and Basilicata, razing tens of thousands of houses to the ground and leaving three thousand dead and 8,852 wounded under the ruins. The inhabited centers of 36 towns were completely destroyed and those in 280 were seriously damaged. The area was incredibly farflung and the weather particularly bad. All divisions available in the area immediately intervened. In the following days numerous army, navy and air force units from everywhere in Italy were transferred into the regions. It was a logistic operation of imposing magnitude which presented difficulties of all kinds, including problems of coordination between the center and the outlying areas and between military, civilian and political organisms. Aircraft from the Army, Air Force, Navy, Carabinieri, Guardia di Finanza, fire-fighters, with technical and logistic support ensured by the aerial and naval bases and the ships at anchor in the neighboring ports, provided a fundamental contribution in many phases of the rescue operations.

EARTHQUAKE IN THE MARCHES AND UMBRIA

In the early hours of September 26, 1997, a strong earthquake struck Colfiorito, Popola, Cesi, Serravalle di Chienti, Assisi. Serious damage and destruction took place in many towns in Umbria and the Marches: Foligno, Camerino, Castelraimondo, Fabriano. Many buildings collapsed, many houses were declared unsafe. The Armed Forces immediately came to the aid of the population.

THE FLOOD IN THE AREA OF SALERNO

On May 5, 1998 insistent rains brought on a state of emergency in the triangle between Avellino, Caserta and Salerno. The province hardest hit was Salerno where a torrent of water and mud moved in on Sarno, Quindici, Siano in Campania with the death of 137 persons while several hundred had to be evacuated. The army immediately intervened in the flooded zones.

THE COMMITMENT FOR THE MAINTENANCE OF THE PUBLIC ORDER

The Italian Armed Forces have also been actively involved, beginning in 1992, in Sardinia against banditism (Operazione Forza Paris); in Sicily in the fight against organized crime (Operazione Vespri Siciliani); in Calabria (Operazione Riace); in Naples (Operazione Partenope) again against organized crime. Since 1995 they have been active in controlling illegal immigration in Puglia (Operazione Salento).

above:
Longarone, October 9, 1963. Alpine troops and Carabinieri on the site of the disaster.
(Historical Bureau of the General Headquarters of the Carabinieri Corps, Rome

Vajont 1963. Italian Army personnel arrive to give aid in the sites of the disaster.
(Army General Staff – Cine-photo television and exhibition production agency, Rome)

FLORENCE, 1966
Carabinieri and army personnel transporting flood victims on an armored M113 troop transport vehicle. The amphibious characteristics of this vehicle were particularly useful at this time in bringing aid to the civilian victims of a natural calamity.
(Army General Staff – Cine-photo television and exhibition production agency, Rome)

preceding page:
FLORENCE, 1966.
Army personnel rescuing the books of the Biblioteca Nazionale in Florence.
(Army General Staff – Cine-photo television and exhibition production agency, Rome)

GIBELLINA IN THE VALLE DEL BELICE, 1968.
A vice-brigadier of the Carabinieri among the earthquake rubble.
(Historical Bureau of the General Headquarters of the Carabinieri Corps, Rome)

BELICE, 1968. AB. 204
helicopter transporting
foodstuffs.
*(Historical Bureau of the
Navy, Rome)*

BELICE, 1968.
AB.204 helicopter landing in the earthquake area with relief for the population. *(Air Force General Staff: Audiovisual production center – Foto 'Troupe Azzurra', Rome)*

FRIULI, 1976. Personnel
of the National Alpine
Association repairing
earthquake damage to
a house
after the earthquake.
*(Army General
Staff – Cine-photo
television and exhibition
production agency,
Rome)*

FRIULI, 1976.
Military at work in the earthquake area.
(Army General Staff – Cine-photo television and exhibition production agency, Rome)

IRPINIA, 1980. Army
personnel rescuing the
wounded after the
earthquake.
*(Army General Staff –
Cine-photo television
and exhibition
production agency,
Rome)*

***UMBRIA – MARCHE,
1997.*** Italian Army field
kitchen set up to furnish
meals for the victims of
the widespread
earthquake.
*(Army General Staff –
Cine-photo television
and exhibition
production agency,
Rome)*

***UMBRIA - MARCHE,
1997.*** Nursery school
set up by the Italian
Army for the children in
the earthquake areas.
*(Army General Staff –
Cine-photo television
and exhibition
production agency,
Rome)*

Sarno, 1997. Army personnel digging in the rubble in search of flood victims or survivors. *(Army General Staff – Cine-photo television and exhibition production agency, Rome)*

*following page,
above:*
***Operation Forza Paris,
1992.***
Personnel of the IX Col
Moschin engaged in
control operations of the
territory in Sardinia.
*(Army General Staff –
Cine-photo television and
exhibition production
agency, Rome)*

***Operation Vespri
Siciliani, Palermo.***
Ucciardone Prison. Fiat 66
14 armored car of the
Driving Regiment on
watch around the prison
perimeter.
*(Army General Staff –
Cine-photo television and
exhibition production
agency, Rome)*

***Operation Vespri
Siciliani, 1992.***
Getting off an ACM 90
truck to set up a road
block. *(Army General
Staff – Cine-photo
television and exhibition
production agency,
Rome)*

The Italian Armed Forces on the International Scene

The Italian military forces, pigeonholed in the circumscribed and subaltern role assigned them by NATO, which in exchange guaranteed Italy a position in which she could enjoy safety, have long resigned themselves to a marginal position. In the course of the 1970s and 1980s, after decades of closure/exclusion, the Armed Forces were touched by the effects of the youth protests, while the Euromissile crisis forced the Italian political powers found themselves face to face with new problems.

The fall of the Berlin wall, at the end of the 1980s, which symbolically represented the end of Soviet hegemony in Europe and the subsequent dissolution of the Warsaw Pact and the dismembering of the Soviet Union - profoundly modifying the international situation - revolutionized the strategic balance and relations between the States. In Italy the new state of affairs had a positive effect also on certitudes and the obdurate behavior that had become a matter of course.

The new strategic situation in the world, which had changed radically in only a few months, redefined the role of the Armed Forces.

Up to 1989 - in a world divided into areas of influence - the two superpowers autonomously managed the conflicts. From that date on however, while the crises and local conflicts increased, the international need and willingness to try and resolve them also grew.

Before 1990, peace-keeping as stated in chapter VII of the United Nations Charter, had been rarely used. In the last ten years the missions of peace have increased and have changed in nature. Previously the purpose of intervention was to reinforce peace or a truce and in agreement with both parties, such as in Lebanon and in the Sinai. Interventions are now carried out when the crisis arises and missions include peace-making and peace-enforcement, next to the traditional tasks of interposition and monitoring.

In 1997 the Security Council entrusted Italy, first country in Europe, with the leading role in the peace operations in Albania. Currently command of the international forces in Kosovo, under the acronym KFOR, has been entrusted to an Italian general.

HUMANITARIAN INTERVENTIONS OF THE ITALIAN ARMED FORCES ABROAD

The Italian Armed Forces have a long tradition of activity abroad. Mention can be made of the intervention of Italy in the crisis in Crete, with the participation of the Royal Navy and the deployment on the island of detachments of infantry and Bersaglieri from 1897 to 1906. The local gendarmes were trained by the Carabinieri.

Here however we intend to limit ourselves to interventions in the second half of the twentieth century.

In the 1950s the Italian Armed Forces were called in to ensure internal order in Somalia and to train the local Armed Forces in the phase of transition towards independence which was proclaimed on July 1, 1960.

The civil war that broke out in the Congo in the summer of 1960 also saw the employment of the Italian Air Force which first evacuated Italian citizens and then brought in food and medicines as well as furnishing support to the U.N. forces striving to bring order to the country. The mission lasted two years, with the massacre of three aviators in Kindu on November 11, 1961.

Among the first humanitarian missions of international fame is the rescue mission of the Viet-

ALBANIA.
MSU AFOR vehicles moving into the Albanian territory. *(Historical Bureau of the General Headquarters of the Carabinieri Corps, Rome)*

namese boat people left adrift in the South China Sea (July 1979) in which the Navy participated with the ships *Vittorio Veneto*, *Andrea Doria* and *Stromboli*.

In 1980, during the terrible civil war which drenched Cambodia in blood, the Military Air Force effectuated an unforgettable air bridge between Bangkok and Phnom Penh, under the auspices of the International Red Cross.

In that same tormented region, 75 Carabinieri, deployed in the various provinces, collaborated in setting up the civil records offices in 1992-93 as part of the UNTAC (UN Transitional Authority in Cambodia) mission.

Lebanon and Sinai

The missions under the aegis of the United Nations began in August of 1979 with the constitution of a multinational U.N. peace force in Lebanon (UNIFIL UN Interim Force in Lebanon) providing for sending an Army and Navy helicopter unit for operations of interdiction in the Gulf of Tiran. This is still in force.

In 1982 another Multinational and Observer Force (MOF) was constituted in the Sinai, again under U.N. auspices. Italian collaboration in the peace operations is ensured by three Navy patrol ships with 90 men, still active with headquarters in Sharm el Scheik. This was one of the first missions in which Italian ships operated outside the NATO area of competence.

From 1982 to1984 the Navy and Air Force were called in for the international U.N. Peace Mission in Lebanon (Lebanon 1 and Lebanon 2) where the more than thirty year mideastern crisis between Arabs and Israelites is still going on.

The newspapers were full of the Italian intervention in the peace-keeping operation in Lebanon. The Italians had a contingent of 2,200 men engaged in patrolling the streets in the ghettos of southern Beirut and controlling the refugee camps of Sabra and Shatila. Lebanese civilians were treated in a field hospital that was always open.

In August of 1984 three minesweepers with the logistic ship *Cavezzale* were sent to the Red Sea, in the zone south of the Suez Canal, for de-mining operations in the sea as a result of a terrorist operation aimed at destabilizing the balance in the Middle East which had already long been in a strong political crisis.

Kuwait

In the summer of 1987, with the intensification of the conflict between Iran and Iraq (attacks on the merchant fleet in the Strait of Hormuz by the Iranian *pasdaran* with small motorboats), the U.N. sent a multinational peace force which included Italy (Gulf 1). From 1987 to 1988 about 20 ships of the Military Navy have been operational to ensure free navigation to Italian merchant ships.

The second mission in the Persian Gulf (Gulf 2) was assigned to the 20th Naval Group in August of 1990, after the emergency deriving from the invasion of Kuwait (August 2, 1990) by the Iraqi military forces.

The ensuing decision of the U.N. to react to the Iraqi aggression in terms of military force shook Italian public opinion which was forced to an awareness that it was impossible to eliminate war. Even a lay standard bearer of pacifism such as Bobbio admitted that "renouncing force in certain cases does not mean doing away with force but solely favoring the force of the bully".

Italy intervened, but the government did not want to use the army. In September it was decided to send a few Air Force Tornado fighter-bombers to the Gulf in the operation Locusta. On January 17, 1991, eight planes of the military Air Force participated in the first war mission in 46 years after the end of World War II. All in all 34 crews and 11 aircraft were deployed.

One plane was shot down and the two pilots were taken prisoner by the Iraqis, prominently featured in the national and international press. In the days to follow the Tornados regularly participated in all the missions assigned.

The following missions were assigned to the Navy:

from September 1990 to January 1991, operation "Desert Shield" to ensure the application of the U.N. resolution regarding the naval blockade from and to Iraq; in the second phase, after the beginning of the "Desert Storm" operation, to provide escort to the aircraft carrier and logistic groups of the U.N. coalition; in the third phase, the Navy units were involved in de-mining with Minesweeper Units.

The Italian missions in the Persian Gulf were the most demanding of those up to then assigned to the Military Navy. The heart-felt commitment for the defence of national interests in zones not normally frequented by Italian ships, far from Italy, bears witness to what the Navy was capable of. In the international field, on the other hand, the efficiency and operative readiness of Italian ships are important unanimously recognized credit cards.

An important consequence of the Gulf event for the Italian Armed Forces was that of eliminating objections, on principle, to the use of volunteers in the services and brought to a head the tendency to replace conscripts with an army of professional soldiers to have a force that could be ready and counted on whenever needed.

KURDISTAN

The end of the crisis of the Gulf in February 1991 coincided with the revolt of the Kurds who hoped to obtain independence taking advantage of the weakness of the Iraqi government. The ferocious repression provoked a massive exodus of the populace. In April the U.N. Security Council intervened. Italy organized the operation **Airone** in which all the Armed Forces participated in furnishing assistance to the Kurdish peoples, and providing the basis for a return to normal conditions of life in the area.

THE YUGOSLAVIAN CRISIS

The 1990s were characterized by the Balkan crisis, which is not yet over, despite the fact that it is now more than a decade that many western nations have been trying to find a solution to this problem bristling with dangerous uncertainties.

In view of its closeness, Italy is directly involved in diplomatic and humanitarian actions aimed at eliminating the negative problems which characterize the involutional process there.

The breaking up of the Yugoslavian Federation and the creation of Croatia and Slovenia as independent nations have cost untold suffering and blood. But the conflict in Bosnia Herzegovina, a multiethnic and multi-religious state, is much more dramatic.

Mention can be made among the many Italian initiatives in this troubled region of the sending of the ship *San Marco* to Dubrovnik (November 1991) with food and commodities for the Croatian peoples. The mission was concluded with the transfer of over 800 Croatian refugees, above all women and children, to the port of Brindisi in Italy, and the constitution of a naval system for the control of the middle and upper Adriatic.

BOSNIA

The crisis in former Yugoslavia irreversibly deteriorated with the intensification of the conflict between Croatians, Serbs and Muslims. The U.N. intervened with a few peace resolutions which essentially called for a voluntary embargo on all merchandise headed for Serbia and Montenegro, with the exception of essential commodities, and on all the arms destined for the Republics of former Yugoslavia.

On the basis of these resolutions an integrated military operation was carried out in which many western countries, including Italy, participated, and which operated in the Adriatic basin to control mercantile traffic directed to the ports of former Yugoslavia and subsequently with a naval embargo against former Yugoslavia, Serbia and Montenegro. The Navy contributed with a fourth of the entire fleet employed.

The conflict in Bosnia lasted three years, ever since the declaration of independence of Bosnia in March 1992 to the signing of the Dayton Peace Agreement in 1995.

In 1992 humanitarian aid had to be sent to the entire territory of Bosnia Herzegovina, in particular the city of Sarajevo and the neighboring area. In this operation an Army helicopter and a G-222 transport aircraft of the Military Air Force were shot down. The two Italian crews lost their lives.

Up to August of 1995 the Italian contribution to the military operations in former Yugoslavia was limited to logistic support and to Sharp Guard. Between then and the end of the year the Italian military planes effected a long series of patrol and reconnaissance flights over Bosnia Herzegovina.

Following the peace accords negotiated in Dayton, the mandate of the multinational operation UNPROFOR (U.N. Protection Force) ended and was replaced by IFOR (NATO-led Implementation Force) (which began on December 21, 1995) and then by SFOR (NATO-led Stabilization Force) (beginning in December 1996). The aims of the international community are to impede resumption of the conflict in the hopes that conditions for a civil cohabitation between the parts can mature.

For the United Nations, the Bosnian crisis meant an acknowledgement of the changes in the world situation and the need to adapt objectives and structures with this in mind.

ALBANIA

The Balkan crisis was and also is the crisis of the Albanian people who found themselves in a desperate situation. Italy as a bordering nation was one of the first to answer the call for humanitarian aid.

After the first massive exodus of the Albanian population towards Italy, in September 1991 the ITALFOR **Pellicano** operation got under way. Almost fifty years had gone by since the Italian Armed Forces had been in Albania, and they were now returning, but this time unarmed, committed to a gigantic humanitarian mission to bring assistance, food and medicines to help the Albanian populations, above all in the hinterland, survive. Thanks to the operation **Pellicano**, which lasted 804 days, the Country of the Eagles could take its first steps towards a democratic transition.

In 1997 civil and institutional disorder in Albania took on new preoccupying proportions and made it necessary to evacuate Italian and some foreign citizens with Italian naval units and helicopters. The operation continued with participation in the Multinational Protection Force (MPF), decided by the EU Council of Ministers and authorized by the U.N. Security Council, aimed at recreating conditions of safety and the return to institutional normality in Albania. The operation known as **Alba** was entrusted to Italy which assumed full command for the first time since the international peace missions began.

The Navy and the Air Force furnished transportation and logistic and operative support for the Italian army land forces with an aliquot reserved to the *San Marco* Battalion. The Carabinieri have been assigned the task of observers, security and control of the territory. Their activity is a model of intervention, used to constitute the Multinational Specialized Unit (MSU) employed in other operations in the Balkans.

Operation **Alba** was an important test-bed for Italy. Achieving the objectives meant renewed international esteem and respect for the nation. The new tasks entrusted to the Italian Armed Forces made it necessary to create, in 1997, the Comando Operativo di Vertice Interforze dello Stato Maggiore Difesa (COI) (Interforce Summit Operative Headquarters of the Defence Staff) to permit the chief of staff to exercise effectively his functions as Chief of the Armed Forces.

Cooperation between Italy and Albania continues in the military field with the NATO program *Partnership for Peace* for the reorganization, technical assistance and training of the Armed Forces. Representatives of the four branches of the Armed Forces are members of the Italian Delegation of Experts (D.I.E. Delegazione Italiana di Esperti). The Carabinieri participate in the Multinational Advisor Police Element (MAPE), the WEU mission for the training and democratization of the Albanian police. The Air Force, with the mission *Albit*, collaborates in the restructuring of the flight training school of the Albanian air forces. The Italian Navy with the 28th Naval Group, deployed in Durazzo, covers the Albanian coasts in an attempt to limit illegal immigration to the coasts of the peninsula and to help reconstruct the armed forces in that country. In the Lower Adriatic a deep-sea naval unit is also deployed and entrusted with the task of discovering and localizing suspect motor-boats and sea craft.

The Italian Armed Forces are part of the NATO logistic Command COMMZ(W) in charge of providing supplies to the allies through Albania.

SOMALIA

In the second post-war period Italy held the administration of the former colony in trust, on U.N. mandate. The Italian Armed Forces, of the Security Corps for Somalia, were called on to ensure internal order and to train the local armed forces in the transition phase towards independence which was proclaimed on July 1, 1960.

Between December 1992 and 1995 Italy was called in three times to operate in the Horn of Africa, to resolve the Somalian crisis which broke out after the fall of Siad Barre and the subsequent taking over of power of the opposing factions of Aidid and Ali Mahdi. The crisis has witnessed thousands killed in the civil war between the two "war lords" which has literally brought the entire nation to the verge of famine. The principal clashes took place in the capital Mogadishu and in the neighboring cities located to the south and north. The U.N. decided to send a multinational peace force (Restore Hope) which, after vain attempts, left the situation more or less as it was. This was the first intervention of "armed humanitarian interference" undertaken without the assent of the nation involved.

The lesson of Somalia was very clear: in the words of Ambassador Fulci, "the United Nations cannot impose peace by making war".

The participation of an Italian contingent, which had been opposed by the Americans, finally took place with the **Ibis** mission which involved several thousand men. The Air Force furnished means of transportation, guaranteed communication links and protected the routes for humanitarian aid. The Navy remained in the area with the ships of the 24th Naval Group, furnishing support to the land operations as well as medical and logistic assistance, while the San Marco Battalion operated on land with the army forces. The Army and the Carabinieri have done their best in carrying out the tasks entrusted them, with considerable losses.

MOZAMBIQUE

Mozambique was the theater of a disastrous civil war which required the intervention of the U.N. to control the cease fire, the demobilization of the Armed Forces and a program of economic and health care for the refugees. Italy intervened in December 1992 with the operation **Albatros** which terminated at the end of 1994.

It is thanks to the diplomatic action of the Comunità di S. Egidio that the conflicting parties finally agreed to sign an agreement in Rome.

KOSOVO

The strong tensions in Kosovo between the ethnic Albanians and the Serb forces came to a head in actions of war which led to a massive exodus of refugees towards Albania and Macedonia. NATO intervention of March 1999, in line with the U.N. resolutions, was addressed to aerial surveillance of the territory and aid to the populations and the humanitarian organizations.

In the 78 days (March 24-June 10) of the NATO aerial campaign against the Serb forces in Kosovo and the Yugoslav Federation, the Italian Air Forces participated with various operational units. Bombing missions of objectives in hostile territory, ensuring the defence of the Italian air space and with missions of support to aerial operations (transportation, reconnaissance, electronic war, SAR - Search and Rescue) were carried out.

All the Air Force missions left from bases located in Italian territory, bases which, among others, ensured the logistic and operative support to most of the air forces of the other NATO countries in the area.

At the end of the war operations, the management of the airport of Pristina was entrusted to the Italian Air Force - for a year beginning with June 1, 2000. In August of the previous year the Italian Air Force had already been charged with the rebuilding of the airport of Djakovica where personnel, material and means destined for the KFOR troops stationed in the theater will be discharged.

The Navy played an important role in the humanitarian operations connected with the mass exodus of refugees from Kosovo to Albania. It actively participated in the operation 'Dinak' (Difesa nazionale per il Kosovo - National Defence for Kosovo) to prevent Serb retaliation against Italian territory, after the NATO aerial raids on Serbia, and the 'Allied Force' operation with naval units and planes embarked, integrated in the NATO aeronaval system. For the first time planes with short take-off and vertical deck landing were used from the mobile aircraft carrier *Garibaldi*.

After the aerial bombing missions were terminated, the Italian countermeasure mine units, together with the NATO forces, were engaged in reclamation operations of the Adriatic waters in the areas where emergencies had required NATO aircraft to dump unused bombs or munitions.

The efforts regarding Kosovo are far from resolving a problem for which no solution seems possible, despite the commitment of the NATO peace mission whose purpose is that of protecting the ethnic minorities in the Kosovar region, in hopes that Serbs and Albanians can once more live together in peace. The soldiers of the Brigata Multinazionale Ovest (MNBW) deployed in Pec, to whom this difficult mission has been assigned, are also entrusted with de-mining, the reconstruction of civil structures, repression of crime, hospital assistance, as well as control of inter-ethnic tensions. The Carabinieri have the difficult task of military police. There are almost five thousand Italians in Kosovo.

Currently Greece, Turkey and Denmark are contributing to the Multinational Brigade under Italian leadership.

At present the command of the international forces in Kosovo, under the acronym KFOR, has been entrusted to an Italian general.

EAST TIMOR

The humanitarian intervention in this Pacific island, 16,000 kilometers from Europe, was determined by the massacre of the Catholic part of the population by the pro-Indonesian paramilitary Muslims.

The multinational force charged with acting on U.N. mandate (INTERFET) was composed of Italy, France, Great Britain, Portugal, under Australian command. This task force moved outside of the traditional alliance system, in absolutely exceptional conditions of climate and hygiene. Paratroopers from the *Folgore* Brigade including a few detachments of the 9th *Col Moschin* Assault Regiment and the Carabinieri of the *Tuscania* Regiment participated in the operation *Stabilise*. The Navy sent the transport and landing ship *San Giusto* with helicopters aboard and a nucleus of commandos and riflemen of the *San Marco* Battalion.

The Air Force participated with two G-222 of the 46th Air Brigade of Pisa. All in all 600 men representing all the Armed Forces.

OPERATION BOAT PEOPLE, 1979.
Navy personnel rescuing Vietnam refugees in the South China Sea.
(Historical Bureau of the Navy, Rome)

In February 2000 this effort also was terminated, which had begun the preceding September, a hard test for the efficiency and organization of support to our contingent in the furthest region in which it was active.

It was evident to all, on this occasion, that the objective of the peace force is not victory but the reestablishment of conditions in which conflicts can be resolved with non-violent means. This is why Italy can be proud of its significant contributions to the international peace operations.

Humanitarian missions in countries at war, in which the participants do not recognize the rules of international politics and do not intend to follow those imposed by the peace contingents, also however begin to pose problems of opportuneness and feasibility. In August 2000 it was decided to interrupt the mission to Timor because it was too dangerous.

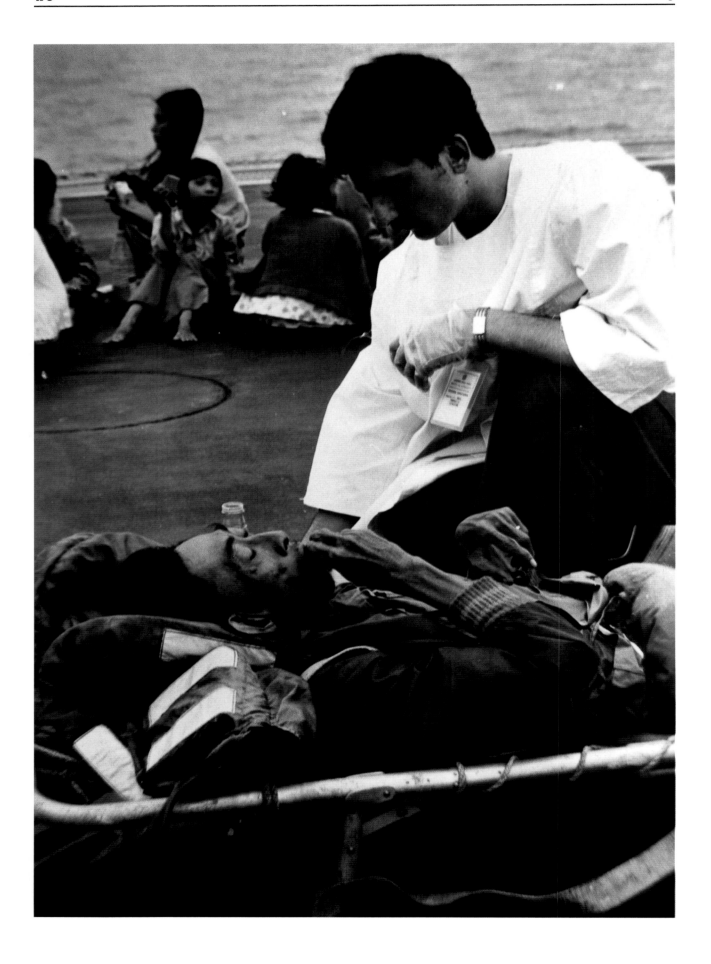

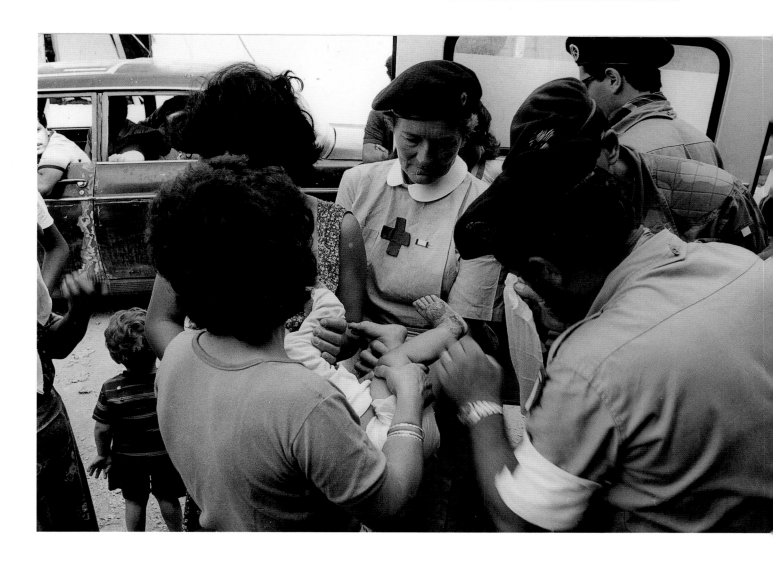

preceding page:
**OPERATION BOAT
PEOPLE, 1979.**
Navy medical personnel
treating Vietnam
refugees.
*(Navy General Staff,
R.E.D.A.P. Office, Rome)*

**LEBANON, ITALCON,
1982.** Nurses and
doctors provide medical
treatment at refugees
centers.
*(Army General Staff –
Cine-photo television
production and display
agency, Rome)*

LEBANON, ITALCON, 1982. American LVTP 7 amphibious landing armoured vehicle armed with a heavy 12,7 mm. M85 SPRINGFIELD machine gun.
(Navy General Staff – R.E.D.A.P. Office , Rome)

Lebanon, ITALCON, 1982. Patrolling through the districts of Beirut, in the Moslem sector. The jeeps are equipped with MG 42/59 machine guns and Rv-3 and Rv-4 radio stations.
(Army General Staff – Cine-photo television production and display agency, Rome)

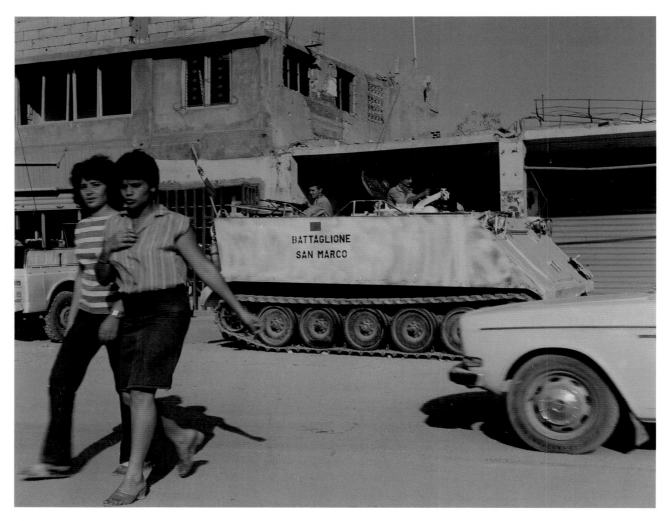

above:

LEBANON, ITALCON, 1982. M113 troop transport vehicle manning a road intersection in the Arab sector of Beirut. The soldiers are armed with MG42/59 and AR70 rifles. Unlike the other Western expeditionary forces, the Italians were the only ones to paint their vehicles white. *(Historical Bureau of the Navy, Rome)*

LEBANON, ITALCON, 1982. A 'Tuscania' paratrooper controls the entry to the Muslim sector in Beirut. The destruction caused by the civil war is all too evident. The weapon in use is a NATO 7.62-mm MG 42/59. *(Historical Bureau of the General Headquarters of the Carabinieri Corps, Rome)*

SINAI, 1982.
Navy coastal patrollers in the Red Sea. These are old wooden-hulled mine-sweepers that were converted into coastal patrol ships. *(Navy General Staff R.E.D.A.P. Office, Rome)*

SUEZ, APRIL 1987.
De-mining operation in
the Suez Canal. The
sailors in the dinghy are
standing guard to
protect submerged
divers.
(Historical Bureau of the
Navy, Rome)

following page:
GULF WAR, 1990-91.
Navy personnel
deployed on exercises
relative to embargo
control operations
during the mission
in the Gulf.
(Navy General Staff
R.E.D.A.P. Office, Rome)

right:
GULF WAR, 1990-91.
Operation Locusta. An
Air Force 'Tornado' in
operative flight over the
desert.
*(Air Force General Staff:
Audio-Visual Production
Center – Foto 'Troupe
Azzurra', Rome)*

GULF WAR, 1990-91.
Putting to sea the MIN
radio-controlled mini
submarine to find and
destroy mines.
*(Navy General Staff
R.E.D.A.P. Office, Rome)*

left:
GULF WAR, 1990-91.
The crew of a 'Tornado' back from a mission. During the 40 days of hostilities, the Italian fighter-bombers carried out a total of two hundred and twenty-six sorties, with the loss of only one aircraft.
(Air Force General Staff: Audio-Visual Production Center – Foto 'Troupe Azzurra', Rome)

GULF WAR, 1990-91.
Air Force specialists on one of the 'Tornados' deployed at the base of Al Dhagra, in the United Arab Emirates.
(Air Force General Staff: Audio-Visual Production Center – Foto 'Troupe Azzurra', Rome)

left and below:
GULF WAR, 1990-91.
The frigate 'Maestrale'
surrounded by LERICI-
class mine-sweepers and
the back-up ship
TREMITI.
*(Navy General Staff
R.E.D.A.P. Office, Rome)*

***Kurdistan, Operation
AIRONE, 1991.***
Road block run by the
'Tuscania' paratroopers
of the Carabinieri
battalion as part of
control operations
in the territory.
*(Historical Bureau of the
General Headquarters of
the Carabinieri Corps,
Rome)*

***KURDISTAN, OPERATION
AIRONE, 1991,*** PHOTO
BY ***ANTONIO DE CANDIA.***
Italian Army medical
personnel providing
treatment to the civilian
population of Zago in
northern Iraq.
*(Army General Staff –
Cine-photo and
television production
and display Agency,
Rome)*

KURDISTAN, OPERATION AIRONE, 1991, PHOTO BY ANTONIO DE CANDIA. Entrance of the Italian camp at Zago, in northern Iraq. On guard is a paratrooper sentinel armed with a BM 59 automatic light rifle. *(Army General Staff – Cine-photo and television production and display Agency, Rome)*

***ALBANIA, OPERATION
PELLICANO, 1991-93,***
***PHOTO BY MARESCIALLO
SERGIO QUAGLIANO.***
An Army Air Force
medium CH-47 C
'Chinook' transport
helicopter lands in
inaccessible zones to
provide the population
with food.
*(Army General Staff –
Cine-photo and
television production
and display Agency,
Rome)*

ALBANIA, OPERATION PELLICANO, 1991-93, PHOTO BY MARESCIALLO SERGIO QUAGLIANO.
A column of 3-axle heavy-transport vehicles travelling through Albanian territory to deliver food to the towns and villages, led by a VM-90. The heavily-damaged conditions of the Albanian communications roads made the Italian drivers' task that much more difficult.
(Army General Staff – Cine-photo and television production and display Agency, Rome)

preceding page:
ALBANIA, OPERATION PELLICANO, 1991-93.
Unloading operations of food stuffs during the Pellicano mission, under the supervision of Albanian military personnel. The columns consists of ACM 90s.
(Historical Bureau of the General Headquarters of the Carabinieri Corps, Rome)

ALBANIA, OPERATION ALBA, 1997, PHOTO BY MARESCIALLO SERGIO QUAGLIANO.
'San Marco' LVTP 7 amphibious vehicle of the Navy, deployed in a coastal patrol operation.
(Army General Staff – Cine-photo and television production and display Agency, Rome)

preceding page:
ALBANIA, OPERATION ALBA, 1997.
A VCC-1 of the 'San Marco' Naval Regiment disembarks from an MTM landing craft. Note the rectangular wave-breaker plate in an extended position.
(Navy General Staff R.E.D.A.P. Office, Rome)

ALBANIA, OPERATION ALBA, 1997, PHOTO BY **MARESCIALLO SERGIO QUAGLIANO.**
A129 Mangusta and AB205 army helicopters on reconnaissance flight.
(Army General Staff – Cine-photo and television production and display Agency, Rome)

preceding page:
ALBANIA, OPERATION ALBA, 1997, PHOTO BY **MARESCIALLO SERGIO QUAGLIANO.**
Check-point run by Bersaglieri in a VCC-1 equipped with additional armour-plating. The weaponry consists of an M2 HB 12.7 mm Browning heavy machine gun and 8 76-mm Krauss-Maffei smoke-making launcher tubes.
(Army General Staff – Cine-photo and television production and display Agency, Rome)

above:
ALBANIA, OPERATION ALBA, 1997.
A C-130 Air Force aircraft deployed during the course of operations in Albania.
(Army General Staff – Audio-Visual Production Center, Rome)

ALBANIA, OPERATION ALBA, 1997.
A G-222 Air Force aircraft deployed during the course of operations in Albania.
(Army General Staff – Audio-Visual Production Center, Rome)

SOMALIA, 1992-1995.
A building dating to the
Italian colonial period.
The Italian navy flag and
the 'Winged Lion' of the
San Marco Battalion fly
from the flagpole.
*(Navy General Staff
R.E.D.A.P. Office, Rome)*

above:
SOMALIA, 1992-1995.
G222 aircraft. These transport planes of the 46th Air Brigade proved to be indispensable for supplying materials and provisions, operating always from half-prepared runways.
(Air Force General Staff: Audio-Visual Production Center, Rome)

SOMALIA, 1992-1995.
A VM 90 Light vehicle of the Italian Army being unloaded from an MTM navy landing vehicle.
(Historical Bureau of the Navy, Rome)

SOMALIA, 1992-1995.
An HH3-F helicopter takes off. The helicopters of the 15th SAR troop performed SAR combat operations, as well as transportation and assistance tasks.
(Air Force General Staff: Audio-visual Production Center – Foto 'Troupe Azzurra', Rome)

above:
SOMALIA, 1992-1995.
Patrolling the streets of Mogadishu aboard a VCC1 vehicle. Note the camouflaging and the sandbags for protecting the personnel.
(Army General Staff – Cine-photo and television production and display Agency, Rome)

SOMALIA, 13 DECEMBER 1992, MOGADISHU.
A mechanized column of the Carabinieri contingent of the 'Tuscania' Paratrooper Battalion, consisting of VCC1 armoured transport vehicles, travels the streets of the Somali city. For this mission, the Italian contingent was given desert-type camouflage uniforms.
(Historical Bureau of the General Headquarters of the Carabinieri Corps, Rome)

Somalia, 1992-1995, photo by Antonio De Candia. Radio Ibis in Somalia was the immediate predecessor of Radio West in Kosovo. Similar to the latter, Radio Ibis was used also and above all to communicate with the local population, in addition to permitting the Italian soldiers to enjoy their rare moments of leisure and to keep up relations with Italy.
(Army General Staff: Cine-photo and television production and display Agency, Rome)

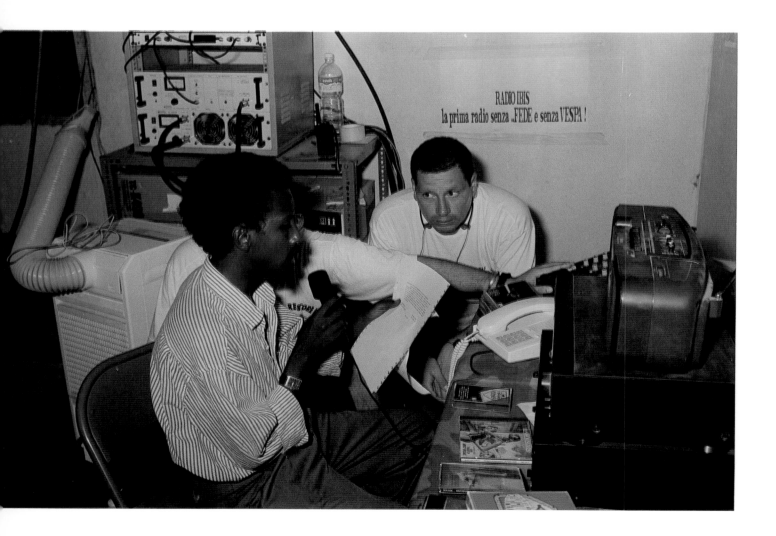

SOMALIA, 1992-1995, PHOTO BY ANTONIO DE CANDIA. An Italian soldier in a Somali school. Our military personnel took care of supplying the local schools with the necessary materials. *(Army General Staff – Cine-photo and television production and display Agency, Rome)*

SOMALIA, 1992-1995, PHOTO BY VITTORIO FALZON.
The capture of an irregular by Italian soldiers in collaboration with the Somali police. The Italian Army committed itself to reorganizing the Somali police force, providing training, weapons and equipment.
(Army General Staff: Cine-photo and television production and display Agency, Rome)

MOZAMBIQUE, OPERATION ALBATROS, 1993.
Position for a machine gun, to protect an Italian encampment. The 'Alpino' is wearing the UN blue cap, and is manoeuvering an MG 42/59 machine gun on a tripod.
(Army General Staff: Cine-photo and television production and display Agency, Rome)

MOZAMBIQUE, OPERATION ALBATROS, 1993.
Control of the territory in the vicinity of a military airport occupied by the Italians.
(Army General Staff: Cine-photo and television production and display Agency, Rome)

Yugoslavia, MOSTAR, 1995. UEOPOL Carabinieri. A gang-way set up over the historic Mostar bridge. The damage suffered by the artistic heritage of the Bosnian city is evident. *(Historical Bureau of the General Headquarters of the Carabinieri Corps, Rome)*

left and below:
**BOSNIA, OPERATION
IFOR, 1996.**
Preparation of a poster
explaining the various
types of antipersonnel
mines and explosive
devices in general. The
prevention campaign
was carried out in the
schools to inform
children of the risks
involved from mines
strewn throughout the
territory.
*(Historical Bureau of the
Army General Staff:
Cine-photo and
television production
and display Agency,
Rome)*

following page:
**BOSNIA, OPERATION
IFOR, 1996.**
'Centauro' heavy
armoured vehicle of the
'Cavalleggeri Guide'
regiment in the streets
of Sarajevo. In the
background, the city
library.
*(Army General Staff:
Cine-photo and
television production
and display Agency,
Rome)*

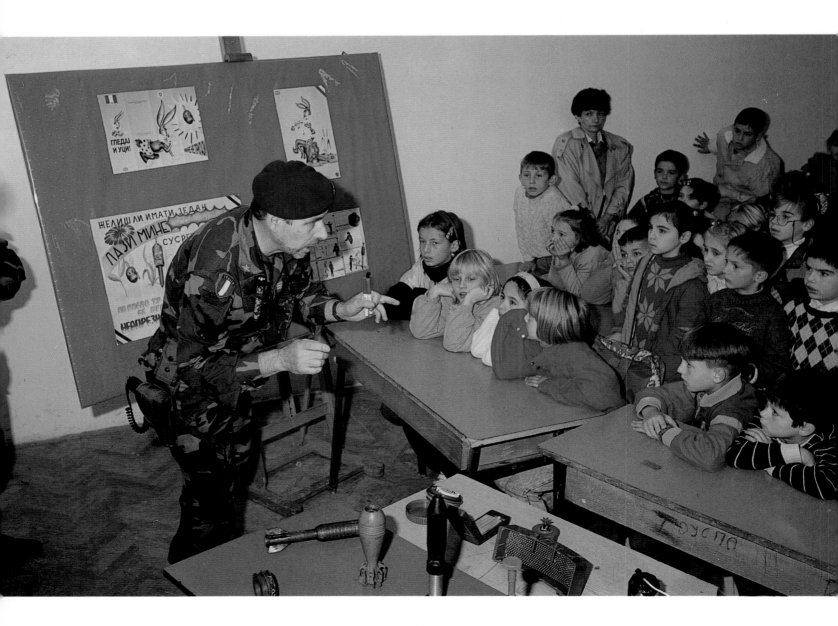

following page:
BOSNIA, OPERATION SFOR 1998, PHOTO BY VINCENZO PEZZOLET.
Carabinieri personnel of the MSU during operations in Bosnia.
(Vincenzo Pezzolet archives)

right:
BOSNIA, OPERATION IFOR 1996.
An Italian motorized column crosses the center of Sarajevo along the so-called and tragically-famous 'Snipers' Boulevard'. In the foreground, a 'Defender' jeep; in the background, two VM 90s, one of which is armoured.
(Historical Bureau of the General Headquarters of the Carabinieri Corps, Rome

BOSNIA, OPERATION IFOR 1996.
Railway Engineers Regiment deployed in restoring a railway line. The Italian detachment is only NATO regiment specialized in reactivating railway lines.
(Army General Staff: Cine-photo and television production and display Agency, Rome)

left and below:
SARAJEVO, OPERATION SFOR (EX IFOR), 1996.
G. 222 and C-130 Air Force aircraft at the Sarajevo airport.
(Air Force General Staff: Audio-visual production Center – Foto 'Troupe Azzurra', Rome)

preceding page:
BOSNIA, OPERATION SFOR (EX IFOR), 1996. Sarajevo. Personnel of the 'San Marco' Regiment deployed in protecting a city street during operations in Bosnia in 1997. In the background, a VM 90 P.
(Navy General Staff R.E.D.A.P. Office, Rome)

KOSOVO, 1999, PHOTO BY GIANCARLO SIMOLA. The city of Pec looked like this when the Italian soldiers arrived there. *(Army General Staff: Cine-photo and television production and display Agency, Rome)*

KOSOVO, 1999, PHOTO BY GIANCARLO SIMOLA.
Discovery of communal graves.
(Army General Staff: Cine-photo and television production and display Agency, Rome)

Kosovo, 1999.
'Bersaglieri' disarm UCK militiamen. The soldiers, armed with mod. 92 Beretta pistols and AR 70/90 rifles wear Kevlar helmets and shrapnel-proof vests.
(Army General Staff: Cine-photo and television production and display Agency, Rome)

Kosovo, 1999.
Refugees embarking
on an Air Force C-130
aircraft.
(Air Force General Staff:
Audio-visual production
Center – Foto 'Troupe
Azzurra', Rome)

EAST TIMOR, 1999/2000,** PHOTO BY **VITTORIO FALZON.
An aerial view of the city of Dili after militiamen had passed through it. *(Army General Staff: Cine-photo and television production and display Agency, Rome)*

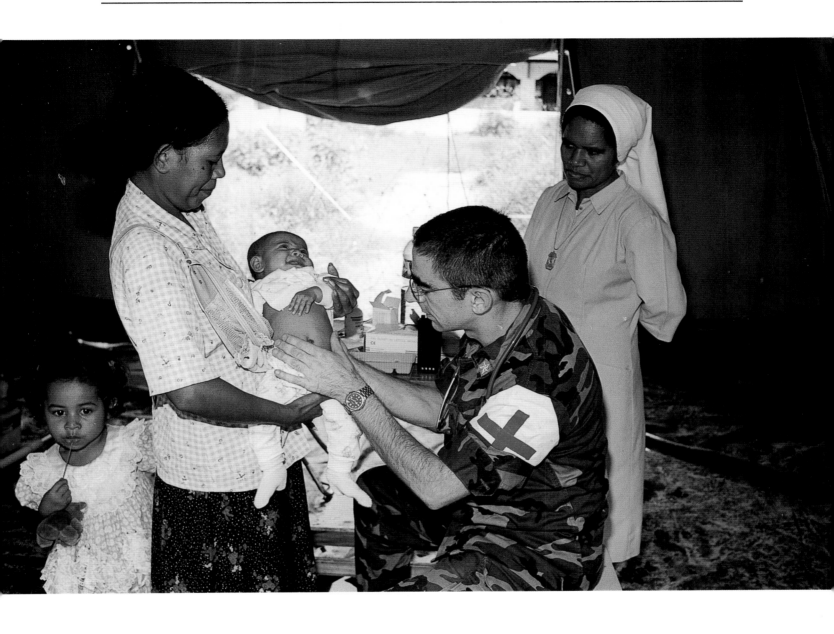

EAST TIMOR, 1999/2000, PHOTO BY VITTORIO FALZON.
The hospital in the Italian camp. Italian military medical personnel provide treatment to the civilian population of Dili. *(Army General Staff: Cine-photo and television production and display Agency, Rome)*

East Timor, Operation INTERFET 2000, photo by Vittorio Falzon.
Control operations carried out by Italian soldiers in the villages of East Timor. The village chief was the point of reference for learning of the difficulties (problems of health, food, or with the militiamen) encountered by the population. The Command was then informed of these, and appropriate steps were taken by way of response.
(Army General Staff: Cine-photo and television production and display Agency, Rome)

EAST TIMOR, OPERATION INTERFET 2000.
As in the case of other out of area operations, in East Timor there was no lack of occasions for socializing between the locals and soldiers. The latter also provided assistance to the former when such was needed. *(Air Force General Staff: Audio-visual production Center – Foto 'Troupe Azzurra', Rome)*

***EAST TIMOR, OPERATION
INTERFET 2000.***
An Air Force G-222
aircraft at the Suai
airport, in East Timor.
*(Air Force General Staff:
Audio-visual production
Center – Foto 'Troupe
Azzurra', Rome)*

***EAST TIMOR, OPERATION
INTERFET 2000.***
An Air Force G-222
aircraft at the Suai
airport, in East Timor.
*(Air Force General Staff:
Audio-visual production
Center – Foto 'Troupe
Azzurra', Rome)*

right:

EAST TIMOR, OPERATION INTERFET 2000, PHOTO BY **VITTORIO FALZON.**
Control operations carried out by Italian soldiers in a village in East Timor. The soldier on the left carries a NATO-supply MINIMI caliber 5.56 mm machine gun.
(Army General Staff: Cine-photo and television production and display Agency, Rome)

EAST TIMOR, OPERATION INTERFET 2000.
Carabinieri of the 'Tuscania' paratrooper battalion control an itinerary. On their heads, the Carabinieri have the headgear appropriate for operations carried out in a tropical climate.
(Historical Bureau of the General Headquarters of the Carabinieri Corps, Rome)

left:
EAST TIMOR, OPERATION INTERFET 2000.
A VM 90 TK vehicle deployed for transporting a squadron of Carabinieri paratroopers of the 'Tuscania'. The vehicle is equipped with protective panels made of composite materials (Kevlar). Note the MG 42/59 machine gun. *(Historical Bureau of the General Headquarters of the Carabinieri Corps, Rome)*

EAST TIMOR, OPERATION INTERFET 2000.
Carabinieri on patrol among the ruins of a village in East Timor, observed with curiosity by a group of local children. *(Historical Bureau of the General Headquarters of the Carabinieri Corps, Rome)*

The Woman Factor

It is said that the only real revolution of the 1900s was that of the women. The Italian woman who began the century without the most elementary rights, moves into the third millennium well aware of her rights and personal duties.

Wars were a powerful factor in bringing about these changes. In World War I women were called in to replace those called to arms in previously inadmissible sectors, above all the war industries. New opportunities were opened in the public administration, the service sector, subsistence. It was to change the makeup of offices and factories.

The first tram conductors and mail-women appeared; tens of thousands of women entered the factories, while the farms were cultivated by other women forced to replace the men at the front in all the productive activities.

In their homes 600,000 women were employed by the government in in sewing military clothing.

The women wrote to the soldiers and provided spiritual comfort, they took care of them as Red Cross nurses. They collaborated with the troops in the hinterland and even in the front.

But women were also leading figures in the popular unrest of 1916 and 1917, both in the country and in the city. In Turin in 1917 a protest for a shortage of bread was turned into a riot led by working class women and laborers.

In Fascist Italy women were still excluded from politics, but were called on to participate in the national project with rights and duties. They acquired a new visibility in the public sphere of sports, mass meetings, free time, but continued to be excluded from many working activities.

Mobilization for the war led to a new acceleration in the construction of a different feminine identity. Women were put in contact with the outside promoting new modes of behavior and new roles, acquiring new skills.

The women once more began working in what were considered male sectors. They were also mobilized in the Armed Forces after radar was installed. A considerable number of female personnel were recruited and trained in the fighter guidance rooms.

After the collapse of September 8, 1943, there were auxiliaries in the Italian Social Republic and, on the other front, women who took part in the war of liberation, in the most varied support activities. In the south, promoted by the Allies, the Female Assistance Corps was constituted in 1945.

On June 2, 1946, for the first time, Italian women could vote for the Constituent Assembly and the institutional referendum, and finally became citizens with full rights.

When all the NATO countries opened the Armed Forces to women in the 1970s, talk of including the women in the military structure also began in the Republic of Italy.

After a long and extremely complex procedure, on September 29, 1999, Parliament voted the Spini law which instituted voluntary military service for women.

In spring of 2000 the first young women participated in the selection for admittance to the Air Force Academy in Pozzuoli, the Military Academy in Modena, the Naval Academy in Livorno.

With the entrance of women, the last barrier between the Armed Forces and society fell. The attention the media paid to the event in its final phases bears witness to the fact that they were aware of the profound transformation that was taking place in the military structures, leading to a professionalization of the Armed Forces and the suspension of the draft.

WORLD WAR I.
War industries. Making hand grenades.
(Historical Bureau of the Army General Staff, Rome)

WORLD WAR I, ITALIAN AMMUNITIONS FACTORY, 1918, PHOTO GIANCARLO DALL'ARMI. 75 mm grenade production line. *(Fratelli Alinari Museum of the History of Photography – Falzone collection, Florence)*

***World War I,
Florence, 1917, Photo
Fratelli Alinari.***
Men and women at
work in the Galileo
factory in Florence.
*(Alinari Archives – Alinari
archive, Florence)*

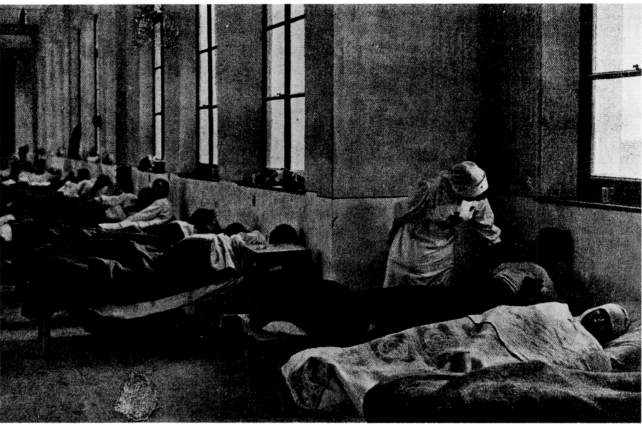

preceding page, above:
WORLD WAR I.
USA war reporters on
the front with a 25 mm
Nordenfelt four barrel
machine gun used by
the Navy in antilanding
operations.
*(Historical Bureau of the
Navy, Rome)*

WORLD WAR I.
Voluntary nurse helping
the wounded in a
hospital behind the
lines.
*(Historical Bureau
of the Army General
Staff, Rome)*

***TREVISO, 1918, WORLD
WAR I.*** Entrenched
camp being built behind
the line of the Piave.
*(Historical Bureau
of the Army General
Staff, Rome)*

WORLD WAR I.
Small group of soldiers
and Red Cross nurses
going along a river on
board a boat furnished
with small cannon,
1915-18.
*(Fratelli Alinari Museum
of the History of
Photography, Florence)*

WORLD WAR I.
Disabled servicemen
helped by Red Cross
nurses in the Roman
Hospital on the Quirinal.
*(Fratelli Alinari Museum
of the History of
Photography, Florence)*

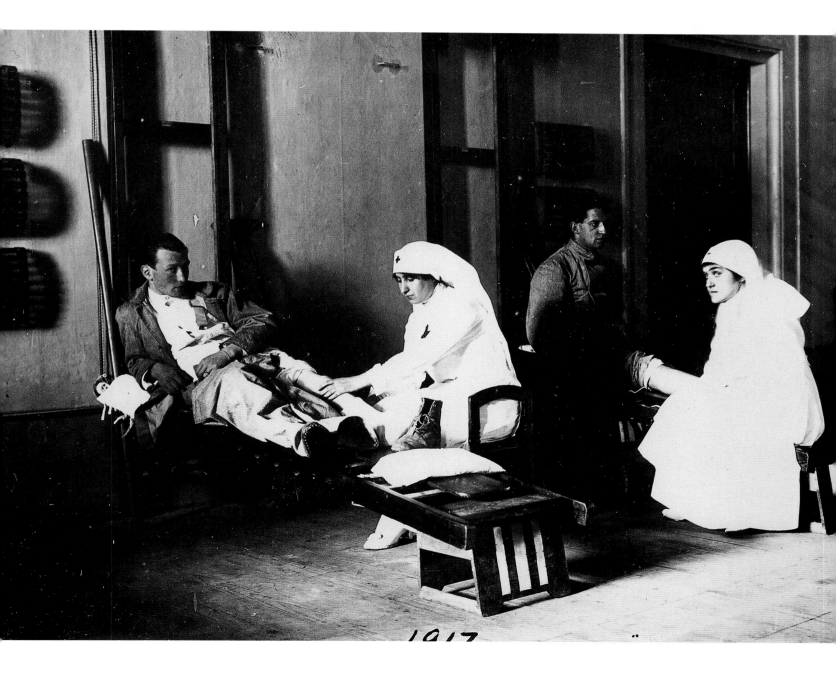

right:
**WORLD WAR I,
MARCH 19, 1917.**
Queen Margherita of
Savoy accompanied by
an Army officer is
welcomed by a group of
Red Cross nurses during
an official visit.
*(Fratelli Alinari Museum
of the History of
Photography, Florence)*

**WAR OF LIBERATION,
MARCH 1945.**
Partisans of the Val
d'Ossola (Novara)
groups. They are
equipped with English
weapons, obtained
through airdrops from
Allied planes.
*(Historical Bureau of the
General Headquarters of
the Carabinieri Corps,
Rome*

left and below:
ROME, 1947.
CAF Assistants at the
inauguration of the
I[st] Course for social
workers at the University
of Rome, 1947.
*(Historical Bureau
of the Army General
Staff, Rome)*

Flight School at Latina, November 2000. A student of the Accademia Aeronautica next to a SIAI Marchetti SF. 260.
(Cine-photo center of the Army General Staff and Photographic Laboratory of the Air Force General Staff, Rome)

left:
AUGUST 2000.
The first female non-commissioned officers in the Italian Navy. They preceded their colleagues in the Army by just a few weeks. *(Naval Academy, Livorno)*

MILITARY ACADEMY OF MODENA, NOVEMBER 2000. Instruction at the firing ground. *(Cine-photo center of the Army General Staff and Photographic Laboratory of the Air Force General Staff, Rome)*

The Anniversary of the Italian Republic

The new relationship between the Italian Armed Forces and civilian society was officially sealed on June 2, 2000. The military parade championed by the President of the Republic Carlo Azeglio Ciampi, a convinced advocate of the recovery of the national memory, of the cult of ideals which form the moral patrimony of the Italians, of the symbols with which the nation can identify, was highly emblematic and included all the sectors of the Armed Forces which in these years have represented Italy abroad in peace operations.

preceding page:
JUNE 2000.
The arrival of the President of the Republic, Carlo Azeglio Ciampi, at the military parade for the June 2nd celebrations.

ROME, 4 NOVEMBER 2000.
The new presidential flag flies from the small tower of the Quirinale.
(Press Office of the Presidency of the Republic, Rome)

June 2000.
The flags of the Italian
Armed Forces go by as
part of the military
parade of the June 2nd
celebrations.

JUNE 2000.
The highest political and
military figures are
present at the military
parade for the June 2nd
celebrations.

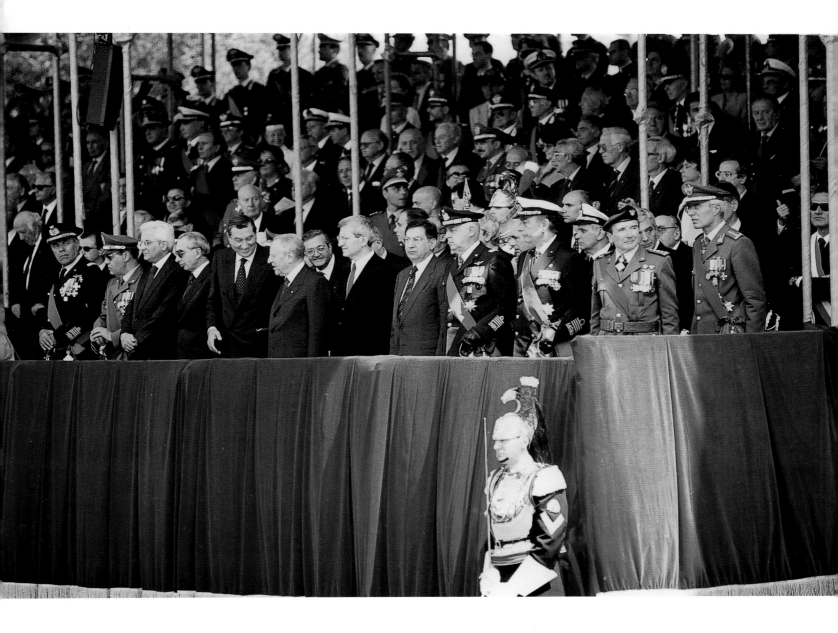

Bibliography

Historical Bureau of the Navy, *La Marina Militare nel suo primo secolo di vita 1861-1961*, Rome, Tip. Regionale, 1962.

Giovanni Alberto, *Storia dell'aviazione*, Turin, Società editrice internazionale, 1973.

Rosario Abate, *Storia della Aeronautica italiana*, Milan, Bietti, 1974.

Massimo Mazzetti, *La politica militare italiana fra le due guerre mondiali (1918-1940)*, Salerno, Beta Edition, 1974.

L'Esercito per il Paese 1861-1975, Rome, Historical Bureau of the General Army Staff, 1977.

Lucio Ceva, *Le forze armate*, Turin, UTET, 1981.

Nino Arena, *La Regia Aeronautica 1939-1943*, General Air Force Staff, Rome, 1982.

Historical Bureau of the General Army Staff, *L'esercito italiano*, Rome, Tipografia regionale, 1982.

Franco Baratelli Micali, *La Marina Militare italiana nella vita nazionale (1860-1914)*, Milan, Mursia, 1983.

Ezio Ferrante, *La grande guerra in Adriatico*, Rome, Historical Bureau of the Navy, 1987.

La Marina italiana, storia di uomini e navi, curated by Arrigo Pecchioli, text by Ezio Ferrante – Franco Gay, Rome, Editalia, 1987.

Giorgio Giorgerini, *Da Matapan al Golfo Persico: La Marina Militare italiana dal fascismo alla Repubblica*, Milan, Mondadori, 1989.

Gianni Oliva, *Storia dei carabinieri: immagine e autorappresentazione dell'Arma, 1814-1992*, Milan, Leonardo, 1992.

Michele Cosentino - Ruggero Stanglini, *La Marina Militare italiana*, Florence, EDAI, 1993.

Alberto Santoni, *Storia e politica navale dell'età contemporanea*, Rome, Historical Bureau of the Navy, 1993.

Gregory Alegi – Baldassare Catalanotto, *Coccarde tricolori. L'Aeronautica Italiana nella Guerra di Liberazione*, Rome, Nuovo Studio Tecna, 1994.

Virgilio Ilari, *Storia militare della Prima Repubblica 1943-1993*, Ancona, Publishing House Nuove Ricerche, 1994.

1992-94 Operazione Somalia, curated by Ruggero Stanglini, Florence, EDAI, 1994.

Alberto Santoni, *Storia e politica navale dell'ultimo cinquantennio*, Rome, Historical Bureau of the Navy, 1995.

Fabrizio Battistelli, *SOLDATI. SOCIOLOGIA DEI MILITARI ITALIANI NELL'ERA DEL PEACE-KEEPING*, Milan, Franco Angeli, 1996.

Oreste Bovio, *STORIA DELL'ESERCITO ITALIANO 1861-1990*, Rome, Historical Bureau of the General Army Staff, 1996.

BOSNIA: L'INTERVENTO MILITARE ITALIANO, curated by Andrea Nativi, Stato Maggiore della Difesa – General Affairs Bureau, 1996.

Luigi Donolo, *STORIA DELLA DOTTRINA NAVALE ITALIANA*, Rome, Historical Bureau of the Navy, 1996.

Gregory Alegi – Baldassare Catalanotto, *NEI CIELI DI GUERRA. LA REGIA AERONAUTICA A COLORI 1940-45*, Milan, G. Apostolo editor, 1996.

Sebastiano Licheri, *STORIA DEL VOLO E DELLE OPERAZIONI AEREE E SPAZIALI DA ICARO AI GIORNI NOSTRI*, Rome, General Air Force Staff, 1997.

Piero Del Negro, *GUIDA ALLA STORIA MILITARE ITALIANA*, Naples, Edizioni Scientifiche Italiane, 1997.

LE FORZE ARMATE DELLA REPUBBLICA ITALIANA 1946-1996, curated by Andrea Buonocore, Rome-Bari, Laterza, 1997.

Pino Agnetti, *OPERAZIONE ALBA. LA MISSIONE DELLA FORZA MULTINAZIONALE DI PROTEZIONE IN ALBANIA*, Stato Maggiore della Difesa - Geographical Institute De Agostini, 1997.

Antonello Biagini, *STORIA DELL'ALBANIA DALLE ORIGINI AI GIORNI NOSTRI*, Milan, Bompiani, 1998.

Giovanni Sabbatucci – Vittorio Vidotto, *STORIA D'ITALIA*, voll. 1-5, Rome Bari, Laterza, 1994-1997.

Alfonso Bartolini – Alfredo Terrone, *I MILITARI NELLA GUERRA PARTIGIANA IN ITALIA 1943-1945*, Rome, Historical Bureau of the General Army Staff, 1998.

A. Laghezza-M.Majorani-R.Salvalajo, *OLTRE L'ORIZZONTE. LE OPERAZIONI ALL'ESTERO DELL'AERONAUTICA MILITARE DAL 1960 A OGGI*, Rome, 1999.

Massimo Coltrinari, *LA RESISTENZA DEI MILITARI ITALIANI ALL'ESTERO. ALBANIA*, Rome, Coremite - Military Magazine, 1999.

Fortunato Minniti, *FINO ALLA GUERRA. STRATEGIE E CONFLITTO NELLA POLITICA DI POTENZA DI MUSSOLINI 1923-1940*, Naples, Edizioni Scientifiche Italiane, 2000.

Mario Isnenghi & Giorgio Rochat, *LA GRANDE GUERRA 1914-1918*, Milan, La Nuova Italia, 2000.

UNMOGIP United Nations Military Observer Group in India and Pakistan	Srinagar Pakistan	from January 1949	UN Mission for control of the truce between India and Pakistan: Italian participation began in 1958
CSS Security Corps for Somalia	Somalia	1952-1960	Control of the territory and public order and training of the Somalian Armed Forces
UNTSO United Nations Truce Super-vision Organization	Jerusalem Israel	from 1958	UN Mission for control of the truce between Arab States and Israel: Italian participation began in 1958
ONUC	Congo	July 11, 1960 June 19, 1962	Sending of provisions and medicines and evacuation of Italian refugees
DIATM Italian Delegation of Techni-cal-Military Assistance	Rabat Morocco	from 1969	Italian mission of advanced training and operation of helicopter pilots
UNIFIL United Nations Interim Force in Lebanon	Naqurah Leban	from June 1979	UN mission for control of the withdrawal of Israeli-te troops from Lebanon
	China Sea	April 4 August 10, 1979	Mission of aid to Vietnamese refugees in the South China Sea
MFO Multinational Force and Observers	Egypt (Sinai) Sharm El Sheik	from April 25, 1982	Observation force on land and sea for the implemen-tation of the 1979 Peace Treaty between Egypt and Israel subsequent to the Camp David agreements of 1978
LIBANO 1 LIBANO 2	Beirut	August 26, 1982 March 6, 1984	UN Mission for the constitution of an interposition force, furnish assistance to the Lebanese government and favor the re-establishment of Lebanese sovereign authority
	Suez Canal	August 22 September 20, 1984	De-mining mission in the Red Sea
Gulf 1	Persian Gulf	1987 - 1988	UN Mission for protection of mercantile shipping and de-mining operation
MIATM - Italian Mission for technical-military assistance	La Valletta Malta	from 1988	Training of the Maltese Armed Forces
UNIMOG	Iran - Iraq	August 16 1988 March 10 1991	
UNTAG United Nations Transition Assistance Group	Namibia	March 30, 1989 April 30, 1990	UN Mission for assistance in the pre-election transi-tional period
UNOCA	Afghanistan	March 30,1989 October 15, 1989	
Gulf 2	Kuwait	August 1990	Application of the UN resolutions n. 660 and 668 for the liberation of Kuwait
Operation Locusta	Kuwait	1990 - 1991	Application of the UN resolution n. 660 for the libe-ration of Kuwait
Desert Shield	Kuwait	September 1990 January 1991	Application of UN resolutions regarding the block-ade to and from Iraq
Desert Storm	Kuwait		
UNIKOM United Nations Iraq Kuwait Observation Mission	Ummqasir Iraq	from 1991 to October 6, 1999	UN Mission for control of the truce in the Iraz-Kuwait border zone
UNSCOM United Nations Iraq Kuwait Observation Mission	Iraq	from 1991	U.N. Mission for control of the application of the UN resolution 688
Airone 1 e 2 Provide Comfort	Kurdistan	May 3 October 9, 1991	Humanitarian assistance to the civilian populations
ECMM European Community Monitor Mission	Bosnia	from 1991	EEC observation mission in former Yugoslavia to control that the terms of the truce agreement are respected. Now operating in Croatia, Bosnia, Fyrom and Albania
UNPROFOR	Bosnia	from March 15, 1992 to December 1995	UN Mission to guarantee the cease-fire between Serbs and Croatians
PROVIDE PROMISE	Bosnia Herzegovina	July 3, 1992 January 9, 1996	Air-landing and air-drop missions for sending huma-nitarian aid to the peoples of Bosnia Herzegovina
SHARP VIGILANCE	Bosnia	from July 10 to November 20, 1992	WEU mission
MARITIME MONITOR	Bosnia	from July 10 to November 18, 1992	NATO mission
MARITIME GUARD	Bosnia	from November 22, 1992	NATO mission
SHARP FENCE SHARP GUARD	Bosnia Herzegovina	from November 22, 1992 to June 19, 1996	NATO mission for patrolling of the maritime routes
DENY FLIGHT	Bosnia Herzegovina	April 12, 1993 to December 20, 1995	NATO operation of aerial patrolling to hinder the warring factions from using aircraft as a military instrument
DELIBERATE FORCE	Bosnia Herzegovina	August 30 September 13, 1995	NATO aerial operation to impose respect of the UNO and NATO injunctions to the Serbs-Bosnians
JOINT ENDEAVOUR JOINT GUARD JOINT FORGE	Bosnia	from December 18, 1995	NATO operations to establish conditions for peace in Bosnia Herzegovina
IFOR Implementation Force SFOR Stabilization Force	Bosnia	from December 15, 1995	NATO mission to consolidate and stabilize peace in Bosnia-Herzegovina and discourage the resumption of hostilities in line with the Dayton peace agreements
UNMBIH-IPTF - United Nations Mission in Bosnia and Herzegovina Internatio-nal Police Task Force	Bosnia-Erzegovina	from December 21, 1995	UN mission for the training and democratization of the Bosnian police
MINURSO - United Nations Mission for the referendum in Western Sahara	El-Aaiùn (Laayoune) Western Sahara	from April 1991	UN control mission in the referendum for the inde-pendence of Western Sahara from Morocco
ITALFOR Pellicano 1 Pellicano 2	Albania	September 1991 December 1993	Sorting, storing and transportation of aid for Alba-nia

ONUSAL	El Salvador	August 7, 1991 October 1, 1995	
UNAMIC - UNTAC	Cambodia	July 23, 1992 July 22, 1993	Setting up of the register of births, marriages and deaths
UNITAF - Restore Hope IBIS 1	Somalia	December 13, 1992 May 3, 1993	UN mission, under U.S.A. command, for the re-establishment of security for the distribution of international aid to the people
UNOSOM 2 - IBIS 2	Somalia	May 4, 1993 March 23, 1994	UN mission for the re-establishment of security for the distribution of international aid
UNCIVPOL	Somalia	1992 - 1994	Control of the territory and maintenance of public order
UNOMOZ Operation Albatros	Mozambique	February 8, 1993 December 27, 1994	UN mission for the re-establishment of security for the stabilization of the country
TIPH 1 Temporary International Presence in Hebron	Palestine	May 8 August 8, 1994	International observers sent to create an atmosphere of mutual trust and security between Palestinians and Israelites resident in Hebron
United Shield	Somalia	January 20 February 28, 1995	
MINUGUA United Nations Mission in Guatemala	Guatemala	from November 1994	UN mission for the verification of human rights
UNAVEM III	Angola	August 24, 1995 June 30, 1997	UN mission
TIPH 2 Temporary International Presence in Hebron	Palestine	from February 1, 1997	Ensure the presence of observers for the consolidation of peace in the Middle East region
FMP - Operation Alba	Albania	March 28 August 11, 1997	UN mission to make the principal entrants points and the seats of the international missions safe in the area responsible for the inflow and distribution of humanitarian aid
GRUPNAV 28 High seas system	Durazzo		Italian mission for control of illegal immigration and the Albanian territorial waters
D.I.E. Delegation of Italian Experts	Tirana	from 1997	Delegation of military experts for assistance and bilateral cooperation in favor of the Albanian Armed Forces
MAPE Multinational Advisory Police Element	Albania	1998	WEO mission for the reorganization and training of the Albanian Police Forces
JOINT GUARDIAN	Kosovo Fyrom (Macedonia)	from October 24, 1998	NATO mission
KVM Kosovo Verification Mission	Kosovo	up to March 20, 1999	Unarmed OSCE observers sent to verify that the cease-fire between Serbian and UCK militias was respected
JOINT GUARANTOR	Fyrom (Macedonia)	from December 3, 1998	Before and during the war operations in Kosovo there was a NATO mission of land forces deployed in Macedonia, in which Italian army units also participated, with the task of ensuring, if necessary, the removal of the OSCE observers in the Kosovar territory (KVM)
EAGLE EYE	air space Kosovo	from November 1998	Allied operation of aerial surveillance
28° Italian Naval Group	Albania		In service for control of the coasts and illegal immigration on the basis of a bilateral Italy-Albania agreement
Albit	Albania		Italian mission to strengthen relations between Albania and Italy. Tasks of safety of the personnel and establishment of a project for the restructuring of the Flight School of the Albanian Air Force
KFOR Kosovo Force	Kosovo	from 1999	Multinational force deployed in Kosovo as part of the NATO Joint Guardian operation
COMMZ(S)	Fyrom	from 1999	NATO logistic command in charge of allied supplies via Fyrom and Greece
AFOR Albanian Force		from April 19 to September 1 1999	NATO mission of assistance to Kosovarian refugees in Albania
COMMZ(W) Communication West Zone	Albania	from September 1999	NATO logistic command in charge of allied supplies via Albania
Railroad Engineers Corps	Kosovo		Reinforcement unit for the re-establishment of civil railroad lines
MSU SFOR Multinational Specialised Units (Joint Forge Italia)	Bosnia	from August 1, 1998	NATO contingent of military police for the control of the territory
MSU-K Multinational Specialised Units	Kosovo	from August 1998	NATO contingent of military police for the control of the territory and maintenance of public order
INTERFET - International Force in East Timor Stabilise	Timor Est	September 20, 1999 February 2000	UN mission to supply humanitarian aid and support in re-establishing the civil institutions
UNMIK United Nations Interim Administration Mission in Kosovo	Kosovo		UN mission responsible for the civil administration and reconstruction of Kosovo
APOD PR - Air Point of dis- embarkation di Pristina	Kosovo	from June 30, 2000 under Italian control	NATO Mission for the control of air traffic and land movements in the airport of Pristina
United Nations Mission Ethiopia Eritrea	Ethiopia Eritrea		
Joint Forge	Bosnia		
UNTAG United Nations Transition Assistance Group	Namibia		Assistance in the pre-election transition period
United Nations Mission in the Democratic Republic of the Congo	Congo	currently being activated	
UEOPOL	Mostar	March 1995-November 1996	Integration of the local Croat and Muslim police

Finished Printing in the month of Dicembre 2000